SANCTUARY

GLOBAL LATIN/O AMERICAS
Frederick Luis Aldama and Lourdes Torres, Series Editors

SANCTUARY

EXCLUSION, VIOLENCE, AND INDIGENOUS MIGRANTS IN THE EAST BAY

Cruz Medina

THE OHIO STATE UNIVERSITY PRESS
COLUMBUS

Copyright © 2024 by The Ohio State University.
All rights reserved.

Library of Congress Cataloging-in-Publication Data
Names: Medina, Cruz (Cruz N.), author.
Title: Sanctuary : exclusion, violence, and Indigenous migrants in the East Bay / Cruz Medina.
Other titles: Global Latin/o Americas.
Description: Columbus : The Ohio State University Press, [2024] | Series: Global Latin/o Americas | Includes bibliographical references and index. | Summary: "Uses interviews and surveys with Indigenous Maya Guatemalans and applies decolonial critical race theory to examine issues of immigration, violence, language, and property as well as white supremacist rhetoric and policy that impact US and transnational Indigenous populations"—Provided by publisher.
Identifiers: LCCN 2024020083 | ISBN 9780814215456 (hardback) | ISBN 0814215459 (hardback) | ISBN 9780814283691 (ebook) | ISBN 0814283691 (ebook)
Subjects: LCSH: Mayas—California—East Bay—Social conditions—Case studies. | Immigrants—California—East Bay—Social conditions—Case studies. | Indians of Central America—Violence against—California—East Bay—Case studies. | Indians of Central America—Crimes against—California—East Bay—Case studies.
Classification: LCC F1435.3.S68 M43 2024 | DDC 305.897/4207944—dc23/eng/20240731
LC record available at https://lccn.loc.gov/2024020083

Other identifiers: ISBN 9780814259221 (paperback) | ISBN 0814259227 (paperback)

Cover design by Laurence J. Nozik
Text composition by Stuart Rodriguez
Type set in Minion Pro

CONTENTS

Preface	*Scarred Family Trees*	vii
Acknowledgments		xiii
INTRODUCTION		1
CHAPTER 1	Citizenship, Economies of Exclusion, and Tech Money	24
CHAPTER 2	Decolonizing Immigration with Critical Race Theory	41
CHAPTER 3	Violence and the Legacy of Colonial Genocide	62
CHAPTER 4	Sanctuary Struggle, Linguistic Discrimination, and Indigenous Displacement	84
CHAPTER 5	Volunteer Literacy Teacher Counterstory	107
CHAPTER 6	Concluding a Story without an End	125
Appendix	*Survey Questions*	131
Works Cited		137
Index		147

PREFACE

Scarred Family Trees

When I first volunteered as an English language teacher at the "Sanctuary," I naively did not expect to conduct research on the current violence that migrants experience or the historical violence of the thirty-six years of "civil war" / *la violencia* that no doubt touched the students and families of students I taught. The space in the pages of this book that I dedicate to the violence and history of violence in Guatemala contextualizes and provides much of the subtext for the interstitial moments I shared with students before class in the church basement, during breaks drinking coffee and eating pan dulce, and in moments before heading out into the East Bay nights from the fall of 2013 to the summer of 2016.

In 2013 I took a postdoctoral fellowship at Santa Clara University (SCU) that paid $45,000 a year. During the move to Santa Clara, my then two-year-old son, William, had a febrile seizure while we were in Southern California that led to him being intubated. When I began volunteering Monday nights at the Sanctuary church, my spouse would worry anytime my son had a fever, which was not unusual given his frequent ear infections. In July 2014 my second son, Jackson, was born right after I was offered a tenure-track position at SCU. I continued to leave at 4 p.m. to drive the two hours in traffic to the East Bay to teach a two-hour class from 6 to 8, followed by another forty-five-minute drive home without traffic, arriving home just before 9. A therapist would later tell me that for partners raising a family, the years dedicated to

vii

parenting small children under the age of five can be among the most difficult times for a marriage.

The exigence for writing this book could be attributed to the argument that "to decolonize, one must first start from within oneself in a reflective process" (Wane 171). The presence of the violence might also be explained by what Oscar Wilde says in *The Critic as Artist* about all criticism being a form of autobiography and therefore be viewed as a part of my late-in-life education about my Guatemalan heritage having found its way into this book's pages. I do not think I will ever know enough about this history, in part because my father's mother, my grandma Dorothy, was separated from her Guatemalan mother, my great-grandmother, as a young girl. Even now, my grandma Dorothy suffers from stroke-related dementia, but even before her short- and long-term memories blurred within her present moments, her mother's history was another lost to fear, secrecy, and shame.

The details are murky as to why my grandma Dorothy's Mexican American father (my great-grandfather Philip) took Grandma Dorothy from her mother and left Dorothy with her aunt Lucy, one of my great-grandfather Philip's sisters. The way the story has been retold in my family, the rationale seems to have been rooted in speculation about my great-grandmother's mental health and her ability to care for my grandmother. Still, this dismissal of her ability to mother could also be an excuse for the tacit acceptance of discrimination against Guatemalans (because my great-grandmother was Guatemalan) that could also be interrelated with gender-based violence (if only the emotional violence of taking a child from a mother). Growing up in Mexican and Chicanx barrios during the 1930s and '40s, in the suburban sprawl east of Los Angeles, my grandmother Dorothy had been taught to feel shame for her mother's heritage. I use "Mexican" to account for those who had recently migrated to the US and "Chicanx" to indicate those US-born people with Mexican heritage. My grandmother mentioned her Guatemalan heritage so infrequently that many family members have even forgotten about these roots of our family tree. Gender-based violence experienced by migrant women and the silences around it contribute to the erasure of family histories and the culpability of the perpetrator of this violence.

My father, Julian, knew the shame that came from growing up in poverty as the oldest of four children and the son of a gardener. Grandma Dorothy had my father Julian when she was eighteen, and when he survived a botched gallbladder surgery during middle school that left him with permanent scars that crisscrossed his stomach up to his chest, she saw it as a sign that my father would join the priesthood. My father wore the shame of these scars on top of the shame of being called "panzón" (potbelly) as a nickname because he was chubby as a little boy and was known for carrying a box of animal crackers around with him. He attended a Catholic Santa Barbara seminary during his first couple years of high school, while the rest of my family sacrificed to pay for my father's education, having only sparse meals on an already tight budget from my grandfather's work as a gardener. My father's time in seminary also taught him how men in power can target and victimize others, possibly even those whose bodies were already marked with physical scars of trauma. These lessons learned on the body and in the mind could be considered representative of what Romeo García calls "haunting," or "that which I could not see, but that stained and coinhabited my memory and body" (232). These hauntings of colonial legacies are often erased when extolling the benefits of assimilating dominant literacies.

My father's time in seminary prepared him to excel when he returned to his high school back home. Not only was he the first in his family to attend college, but he also earned his master's degree in English; the attainment of this degree can be seen as providing the promise of social mobility often associated with a high degree of literacy, demonstrated by the power to transform my family's work from gardening to the teaching of college English. I often leave the impact of my father's seminary education at that, letting the sleeping ghosts of abusers lie. In my father's death in 2006, I recognize the hauntings of violence and the lingering trauma, and now I am "working with those who cannot be heard and seen in and on their own terms" (Romeo García 234). My father faintly alluded to the abuse he experienced in seminary before he died, but in much the way that I come to terms with violence in the following chapters, I turn to sites where these hauntings have been captured in text. In a 2019 article from the *Santa Barbara Independent* newspaper, the evil of my father's time in the seminary is documented quite plainly: "The Archdiocese of Los Angeles and the Catholic Church's western Jesuit province self-published a list of 200 clergymen accused of child molestation, 12 of whom held lengthy postings in Santa Barbara dating back to the 1950s" (Hayden). My father's traumas triggered our familial predisposition to a disease that caused him to later seek sobriety after self-medicating for much of his life. I can only speculate how much time was spent grappling with the hauntings of the seminary.

Some of the reasons I began volunteering at the Sanctuary also came from having been hired at a private Catholic university. After I graduated with my PhD from the University of Arizona in 2013, a postdoc at Santa Clara University helped me return to California from Arizona, where anti-Latinx legislation such as Senate Bill 1070 called the citizenship of all Latinxs into question. But my desire to volunteer was also rooted in an awareness of class and educational privilege. When I was young, I remember watching a college football game with my father, who told me to root for the public school playing against the private school. "We're public-school people, son," he told me. His working-class ethos was evident when, as a community college instructor, he would take me around his school and introduce me to all of the secretaries and office assistants prone to the pretensions of some of his colleagues. I believe it was from this very same ethos that I approached classes at the Sanctuary, grateful to the students for taking it upon themselves to come to evening classes and learn despite being excluded from traditional educational spaces.

In keeping with my autobiographical criticism, I am drawn to critical race theory because of my family's history with racism, particularly my white mother's disownment by her father when she married my Chicano father (Medina, "Digital" and "Family"). I am also drawn to decolonial methodologies, which allow me to see the colonial hierarchies discriminating within my Latinx heritage, imposing religious doctrine and distorting relationships with language, to name a few. My decision to write this preface stems from an Indigenous belief in stories as knowledge-building and an understanding that my Latinx family's origin story is a part of the messiness and transparency of decolonial work: "By talking about and modeling transparency regarding the complexities we've faced as scholars attempting to do decolonial work, we provide space for other scholars to acknowledge and . . . rectify the messiness involved in their own work" (Itchuaqiyaq and Matheson 21). A pressing and long-standing concern about Latinx rhetorical scholarship is the narrow focus on Mexican and Mexican American histories and culture. If my own family history teaches me anything, it's that we as Latinx scholars might very well have inherited this exclusionary view through the ways in which heritage from Central and South America has been erased within our own homes. Decolonial work also holds the promise of new worlds that we have yet to imagine.

In this book, I identify as Latino as a cisgendered person of Mexican, Guatemalan, and European white heritage, although I sometimes also identify as Chicano because my Mexican heritage has been centered by my family and many mainstream discussions of Latinx identity in the US. I use "Chicano" and not "Mexican American" because the latter tends to denote a lack of critical awareness of politics and history in the US. Predominantly, I use the term "Latinx" in plural and singular form to speak of people of Latin American heritage in the US, as an inclusive way of accounting for the many heritages, genders, sexualities, and racial identifications that this diverse population contains.

I in no way mean to make excuses for a field's fixation on the border and the country sharing this border. I acknowledge that many academic genealogies in this subfield stem from Gloria Anzaldúa's work, which drew much-needed attention to the borderlands, *mestizaje,* and the need to water all of our roots. However, I in no small part hope that this monograph will be part of a growing body of transnational rhetorical scholarship on the Americas. The messiness of this research parallels the messiness of the twisted roots, scarred trunk, and brittle branches of my own family tree.

ACKNOWLEDGMENTS

Thank you to the staff and leadership at the Sanctuary church where I spent three years as a volunteer teacher and researcher. I am extremely honored and humbled to have been welcomed into this community. The longer I volunteered, the more I saw how deeply committed you were. Because this book project is so grounded in a specific community, I first have to thank the pastor and staff at the church I call the "Sanctuary." The example set by the staff, who practiced what the Judeo-Christian tradition calls "works" without any expectation or ulterior motive for the people they served, was a continued source of inspiration. I am thankful for the staff who helped me make copies and answered my questions, but more so because they did so while performing the roles of social workers, language program organizers, and church stewards in charge of cleaning and maintaining the aging building. I am also thankful for the students who worked hard to learn English and whose trust with the details of their lives they shared with me. I am grateful for all the other volunteer teachers who gave their time and energy to the students of the Sanctuary, with their various commitments of time and experience levels in teaching.

Thank you to Frederick Luis Aldama and Kristen Elias Rowley at The Ohio State University Press for believing in this book as a part of the Global Latin/o Americas series, coedited with Lourdes Torres. Frederick, you've set an amazing (and daunting) inspiration, as your prolific writing across all borders and genres has taught me a lot about not limiting expectations for the writing we can do, all while supporting scholars from early grad school through mid-career. Shout out to your part-time collaborator William "Memo" Nericcio, whose inventive graphic design and scholarship continue to inspire awe.

Thank you to Santa Clara University and the English Department, which provided me with the time and space to complete the writing of the book manuscript during a sabbatical from teaching. Julia Voss, thanks for taking on the somewhat daunting task of department chair.

Thank you to everyone who read different drafts of chapters at all stages, especially those early rough drafts where I had not quite discovered how I would be able to organize and synthesize three years of notes, experiences, and other information. Thank you to Sonia Arellano for help with thinking through the violence of immigration; I am thankful for your scholarship and friendship. Big shout-out to my academic hermana, Aja Martinez, whose scholarship continues to win awards and attract the attention of people who have never read CRT, though have thoughts. I am grateful for your friendship since grad school through our scholarly collaborations and beyond. Steven Alvarez, mil gracias for your insights on languaging! Thank you to Amy Lueck for your quick turnaround on feedback and insightful suggestions; I hope I did not infringe too much on your sabbatical productivity. Your commitment to memorializing the Ohlone Muwekma Indigenous populations of the Bay Area is greatly appreciated. Thank you, Matt Gomes, for your theoretical thoughts and suggestions; I appreciate your ability to balance the highly theoretical with the tangible realities.

Big shoutout to the Culture Power Difference (CPD) folks here at Santa Clara: Anthony Hazard, Christina Zafagna, Danielle Morgan, Allia Morphis, and Jesica Fernandez. Y'all were generous at the early stages of writing this book. It's hard to believe some of the early versions of these chapters resulted in the version of the book that exists today. I will forever appreciate your patience with how far this project came.

Gracias to the Latinx Faculty Group here at SCU. I am honored to spend time with and learn from gente like Francisco Jimenez, Pancho Jimenez, Pedro Hernandez, and the Anas. We are a small but dedicated group of gente who contribute so much to the first-generation students and future educators here.

Thank you to my Kids on Campus parents who have helped navigate being a parent-scholar: Amelia Fuller and Josh Frantz, Kirsten and Kenton Read, Alejandro Masias and Eva Blanco, Erik and Robin Tillman, Caleb and Cat; y'all were the bubble keeping our sanity during the pandemic. Not much writing happened during that period, but we learned that forefronting our humanity is so much more important.

ACKNOWLEDGMENTS · xv

Much love to my NCTE/CCCC Latinx Caucus gente! Big abrazos to Jaime Armin Mejía, who I appreciate being able to call a friend: you are such a mentor to many. I have appreciated your support for this past decade plus. Thanks to Octavio Pimentel, Cristina Kirklighter, Iris Ruiz, Victor Villanueva, Isabel Baca, and Raúl Sanchez for your early support and leadership in the caucus and the field broadly. Much appreciation to José Cortez and Romeo Garcia for your theoretical musings and aspirations to break this reality in hopes of a better one. Alex Hidalgo, thank you for your cinematic eye; my Twitter avatar thanks you. Shout out to Genevieve de Mueller Garcia, fighting out of New York by way of New Mexico. Laura Gonzales, I always look forward to what's coming up next for you and Victor del Hierro, not to mention Marco del Hierro, the other Bodega Boy. Gaby Rios, I'm very grateful for your work, which informs my counterstorying. So many other buena gente who I cannot list!

I couldn't do so much of my work without my former caucus cochair, Christina Cedillo, whose leadership in the field with national service is only rivaled by her editorial leadership with the *Journal of Multimodal Rhetorics,* the many collaborative special issues she's edited, and the many peer reviews she provides the profession.

Much love to Ersula Ore, David Frank Green, and Damon Cagnolatti for letting me tag along with your writing group, even though I've probably talked and imbibed more than I've ever actually written with y'all. Donnie Johnson Sackey, I always enjoy our conference moments. Shout-out to Docta Elaine Richardson for being an inspiration to write fearlessly about our pasts. Thank you, Adam Banks, for your continued inspiration in scholarship and on the bird app.

I need to send a big shout-out to Angela Haas, one of the most influential thinkers on decolonial practices who has influenced my work and been a big advocate during my early career. Thanks to Andrea Riley Mukavetz and Lisa King for your research that continues to inform my thinking in important ways.

To all of my Arizona Wildcat network, bear down! Kenny Walker, thank you for our continued collaborations—I learn so much from you. Damián Baca, Cristina Ramirez, and Adela Licona, thank you for helping me through my grad school journey and up through my early career to my present, posttenure liminal space. Anne-Marie Hall, thank you for challenging me to continue considering my pedagogical activities and outcomes. Thank you to my grad folks: Jerry Lee, Ashley Holmes, Crystal Fodrey, Faith Kurtyka, Cassie Wright, Erica Cirillo McCarthy (we miss you up here), Rachael Wendler Shah, Katie Silvester, Roseann Carlo, Tom Do, Brad Jacobson, Eric House, Marisa Juarez, Amanda Wray, and Elise Verzosa.

Thanks to the Texas State crew, though y'all have graduated and moved out of central Texas: Justin Whit, Casie Moreland, and Elisa Crowe.

SCU English Department folks who read early drafts, thank you: Kirstyn Leuner, Juliana Chang, Andy Garavel, Mariyln Edelstein. Thanks to Simone Billings for having my back all along my journey here from applicant to post-doc to the tenure-track position. Phyllis Brown and Michelle Burnham, thank you for the leadership, especially on the search committees we've collaborated on. I appreciate Heather Turner's cutting-edge knowledge of TikTok, which is helping me not to feel too old too quickly. Shout out to Kai Harris and Daniel Summerhill: it's been great to see your star on the rise as I was writing this.

I am forever grateful to SCU's Ignatian Center, with whom I traveled with other faculty and staff to the US-Mexico border and listened to the stories of migrants at the Jesuit-run Kino Initiative. Hearing the experiences of people caught in the broken immigration system is both heartbreaking and necessary if we are to imagine a different world.

Thanks to my Bread Loaf colleagues: Damían Baca, Jeff Nunokawa, Langdon Hammer, Ruth Forman, and James Chase Sanchez. And thanks to Bread Loaf students Rex Lee Jim, Denny Gonzalez, and all the Loafers who value the joy of a life of letters and practice intellectual curiosity with great enthusiasm.

Thanks to AKA Sunnyvale One World jiujitsu and the morning crew at Caio Terra Association, where I was able to work out nervous energy in the predawn hours doing Brazilian jiujitsu before settling down to write. The parallels between developing a disciplined martial arts habit and a consistent writing habit are perhaps something I will have to dedicate some research time to in the future.

So much gratitude and appreciation to my partner, Kathryn, who at the time of my volunteering at the Sanctuary took care of our three-year-old (while also pregnant) on Monday nights when I drove hours to volunteer in the East Bay and who subsequently took care of both our sons as I continued to volunteer. Thank you, Jackson and William, for inspiring me to work hard and set an example for you both. I love how you both love books and have found your interests in school and have excelled. Thanks for accompanying me to the library, to author book readings, and on dog walks and for going tree climbing with me.

INTRODUCTION

Volunteering is a lot like researching something in that the longer one does it, the more one feels, or is haunted by the feeling, there is more that they could have or should have done. This book brings together research from a period between 2013 and 2016, when I taught English as a second language as a volunteer in the East Bay of Northern California, during the birther claims up through the presidential campaign of Donald Trump. In the following pages, I argue for the ways in which immigration policy and access to education exclude Indigenous migrant populations from Central America, specifically Guatemala, who have already been negatively impacted by US intervention that benefitted transnational business. Under the guise of protecting against the communist threat, the settler colonialism of the US also re-entrenched boundaries between itself and Mexico, Central America, and South America, even though the histories of migration within these geographic places predate European contact. Policy around citizenship brings to light the ways in which people of color have been treated as property and displaced as a part of the United States' erasure of the legacies of American exceptionalism, manifest destiny, and "protecting democracy." Through critical race theory (CRT) and decolonial methods, I highlight the matrices of colonial power interconnected with racism and anti-Indigeneity both inside and outside the US. Dominant narratives about "good" and "bad" migrants support visa systems abused by tech corporations that limit access to migrants seeking refuge from violence at home, and these status quo stories about migrants in education further contribute to beliefs about migrants not caring about education. As a country we cannot continue to blame the victims in a broken system meant to keep migrants in precarious positions as tenuous labor that can be thrown away at any time.

Across the Golden Gate Bridge from the tech industry wealth of San Francisco, hundreds of migrant students participated in varying levels of English language classes at a Spanish-speaking church. I refer to the students as migrants no matter their legal status or whether they are seeking asylum because access to these categories remains in flux, often serving only to exclude. The work at the Sanctuary, in stark contrast, was to include those without traditional access to literacy education, but also, the work of the church staff offered resources related to rent, legal, and spiritual needs. I call this church the "Sanctuary" for purposes of anonymity because of the vulnerable population of adult migrant students in the English program and congregation whose citizenship statuses varied. I chose the term "Sanctuary" partly because the church and pastor became publicly active when Trump came into office, but more importantly, because of the work I observed by the staff at the church. This work included helping members of the church secure food and housing, while allowing unhoused people to sleep along the outside of the church, embodying a space in which to seek refuge. Sanctuary also provides a guiding concept around which critical race theory and decolonial theory are grounded as they serve to elucidate the reasons for seeking refuge and continuing to struggle for this space.

When I began volunteering, President Barack Obama had already been referred to as the "Deporter-in-chief" "for overseeing three million deportations" (Walia 59). This number, though, has been shown to be inflated by repeated deportations of the same individuals. Shortly after my time at the Sanctuary, Donald Trump became president of the United States, ratifying xenophobic immigration enforcement and prompting some cities, university campuses, and churches to declare themselves as sanctuaries against these executive orders. Instead of simply deporting, as Obama had been known for, Trump separated families and locked up children. The following chapters capture some of the sentiments and perspectives of migrants prior to and during Trump's xenophobic presidential campaign. This period is important because the rhetoric of his xenophobic campaign mirrored the rhetoric and policy of his presidency. The following chapters also address the violence in Guatemala that comes as a result of Trump-like fascism and free market exploitation going unchecked.

INTRODUCTION · 3

This book is about the intersection of citizenship, violence, language, and property affecting migrants from Central America, aspects widely overlooked in the United States. As an examination of exclusionary rhetoric and policy in the US, this book takes us to Christa Olson's call that "rhetoricians working in the United States ought not only look southward when we invoke American rhetorical history but also re-examine U.S. domestic rhetorics with an eye toward Latin America" (264). In my analysis of antimigrant policy in California affecting Central Americans in the US, I highlight the culpability of the US government's interests in causing many to migrate north. But I also ask how the abuse of the visa system by companies in Silicon Valley reinforces categories of "good" and "bad" immigrants. This work builds on those works by rhetoric of immigration scholars who "have found that the meaning-making practices of immigrants can call into question issues of exclusion, including racialized hierarchies of citizenship and the criminalization of immigration" (Ribero, *Dreamer* 10). These US interests contribute to and, in many cases, leave no other option than for migrants to risk their lives by making the journey to the US for an American Dream that many in the US regard critically and as mythical. However, a better life for many from Central America is finding refuge from violence and weakened governments following US intervention.

Many migrant students at the Sanctuary come from Guatemala, which has been directly and indirectly impacted by the political and economic interests of the US traceable back to the supposed spread of communism and continuing all the way up to the beans for Starbucks coffee. In addition to corporate interests in coffee and palm oil, the US government supported Guatemala's government in an attempted genocide of Indigenous Maya, officially referred to as a thirty-six-year "civil war" (Sanford; Torres). A 1999 UN-backed Commission for Historical Clarification official document titled "Guatemala—Memory of Silence" reported that 83 percent of the victims of human rights violations were Indigenous Maya, and 93 percent of those responsible for human rights violations were the state and military (546–47). While the attempted genocide by the Guatemalan government is said to have concluded in 1996, the homicide rate in recent years has continued at rates near those of the "civil war" (Obinna; Taft-Morales), fueled by the drug trade and US drug consumption. Migration from countries like Guatemala, Honduras, and El Salvador remain "inextricable from displacement created by US dirty wars backing death squads" (Walia 39). However, the public relations lauding of migrant labor in Silicon Valley is reserved for the mythical "good" migrants who are the founders and CEOs of multimillion-dollar start-ups, rather than those seeking refuge for the lives of their families.

Through working with adult Indigenous Maya Guatemalan students at the Sanctuary in the East Bay from 2013 to 2016, I came face-to-face with the layers of colonial influence and intervention that continued to impact my students' lives. By colonial influence I speak of those in governmental power in Guatemala who identify primarily with European heritage and who have conspired with transnational business interests to the detriment of the predominantly Indigenous population. Unlike some of the volunteer teachers, I have Spanish languaging abilities that allowed me to translate aspects of lessons into Spanish, and while Spanish is *yet another colonial language,* it has been racialized as spoken by nonwhites with less power in the US. Still, the impact of learned generational secrecy and silence from the Guatemalan genocidal "civil war," also referred to simply as "la violencia" (the violence), created divisions among the Indigenous people who speak twenty-one different Mayan languages, but also within those groups who speak the same Indigenous language. The majority of Maya at the Sanctuary spoke Mam, although I learned that the majority Mam-speaking Maya at the Sanctuary could not communicate with Mam speakers from other regions. Since the supposed end of the "civil war" in 1996, the proliferation of street gangs and narco-traffickers who inherited power from a weakened, ineffectual government continues to perpetuate a culture of mistrust (Green; Ujpán; Zur). Many Indigenous Maya learn from the land and sustain themselves on the corn, beans, and other agriculture they produce from their milpas (Green; Menchú; Ríos). They have been displaced, however, through attempted genocide and transnational land grabs that threatened and continue to threaten their ways of life. In the US, these Maya have exchanged gang and narco-trafficker violence for the dehumanizing rhetoric of political leaders, militarized immigration enforcement, promises of empowerment through literacy, and further displacement from (as a result of) gentrification. My book *Sanctuary* provides a point of entry into the intersectional issue of immigration, using interactions, interviews, and survey data from Maya adult students in the East Bay of Northern California. My intent is to untangle how language and policy serve to exclude those racialized by language and Indigeneity from citizenship, education, and property through critical race theory and decolonial frameworks that center the stories and lived experiences of people of color and Indigenous populations.

When I volunteered at the Sanctuary from 2013 to 2016, very little attention was paid to the issue of Central American immigration in the public political discourse. When Trump became president, a part of his prolific Twitter posts was a message meant to stir up fear in MAGA supporters and offered a stern warning to would-be migrants from the bully pulpit. In 2018 President Trump posted on social media that the caravans of migrants coming from Central

America through Mexico contained MS-13 gang members and Middle Eastern terrorists. News organizations later reported these claims as unsubstantiated and disproven (Kessler et al.). Still, the negative attention from Trump and the awareness raised by the caravans highlight the tension between invisibility and visibility. Latinx rhetoric and disability scholar Christina Cedillo brings this issue to light when explaining, "Invisibility can simultaneously protect vulnerable people and render them susceptible to violence; visibility can invite public support while increasing surveillance and policing" (203). The visibility and policing of these caravans can be seen in Vice President Kamala Harris's 2021 visit to Guatemala, during which she callously told potential migrants, "Do not come" ("Kamala Harris"). In both instances, the office of the president of the US addresses this humanitarian issue with reactionary rhetoric. This rhetoric fails to admit culpability in the factors contributing to the need for youth to leave Central America because of destabilized governments resulting from US intervention that allowed gangs and drug traffickers to seize control (O. Martínez, "Why"). Instead of acknowledging the United States' role in the destabilization of Central American governments under the guise of an anticommunist strategy, Harris's political narrative echoes reactionary "secure our borders" rhetoric while Trump responded with conspiratorial speculation. And in doing so, both offices of the US president continued to ignore how the economic success of the US is built on the exploitation of Latin America. Rhetorics of "secure our borders," "good and bad immigrants," and "learn the language" that make up the US can be traced to how the country positions itself in relation to all of its neighbors to the south. Conversely, rhetorics "we today label 'Latin American' have been integral to the rhetorics of what became the United States" (Olson 265). Vice President Harris's trip to Guatemala shows how the US securing borders against an "immigration crisis" no longer simply means the US-Mexico border, but the borders of countries below Mexico's southern border as well. Harris's rhetoric of "Do not come" also speaks to how "colonialism, genocide, slavery, and indentureship are not only conveniently erased as continuities of violence in current invocations of a migration crisis, but are also the very conditions of possibility for the West's previously guarded imperial sovereignty" (Walia 6). My time at the Sanctuary preceded Trump's and Harris's rhetoric, but this rhetoric has been the same since Eisenhower characterized the Guatemalan government as a communist threat and Reagan rejected refugees from the "civil war" by classifying Guatemalan migrants as "economic migrants," denying the human rights violations taking place during the genocide of Indigenous Maya (Gzesh). The economics of immigration provides additional context for understanding how Harris's rhetoric extends the preceding presidential approach to immigration by

6 · INTRODUCTION

increasing Department of Homeland Security funding: "George W. Bush provided $19.5 billion in discretionary funding to DHS in 2002, and this amount has steadily increased across presidential administrations; under Biden's presidency it has reached $56.7 billion for the fiscal year 2023" (Ramirez 184). Harris's exclusionary approach to rhetorically addressing the topos of immigration perpetuates the commonplace responses issued by presidential administrations that intervened outside of the US on behalf of business interests or, in more recent administrations, continue to invest in the business of fortifying the US border. In doing so, the US continues to rediscover the Americas and dispossess Indigenous Central Americans from crossing through ancestral homelands that have been privatized out of the hands of Meso-Americans.

LEADERSHIP AND STAFF AT THE SANCTUARY

Central Americans were able to find refuge at the church I call the Sanctuary, with the English program where I volunteered existing as a result of the Bay Area's history of being politically active and the history of religious organizations offering aid. In a 2014 *Los Angeles Times* story covering the Sanctuary and other churches offering assistance and resources to migrants in the area, the journalist corroborates this point by stating, "In the Bay Area, where the second-largest group [of Central American migrants] has settled, a particularly robust activism has developed—fueled in part by the region's history as a birthplace of the sanctuary movement of the 1980s to help those fleeing Central American civil wars" (Romney). Before, during, and after the time I volunteered, the pastor at the Sanctuary actively worked with migrants and members of the Spanish-speaking congregation to find temporary housing, food, and resources for those navigating the immigration process. In an examination of collective action by pastors advocating for migrant rights, rhetoric scholar Anne Teresa Demo reminds her audience that "diverse denominations have a long-standing organizational history of aiding refugee resettlement and, increasingly, advocating for the rights of immigrants in local controversies over immigration enforcement" (52). When Trump was elected president in 2016 and signed executive orders empowering the militarization of immigration enforcement, the leaders of the Sanctuary church were among a group of church leaders who publicly said their churches would provide refuge. Composition theory scholar Jens Lloyd acknowledges that at the university level, "the sanctuary campus movement stands out as one of the most ambitious responses to the growing sentiment in the United States" (152). However, Lloyd's concession about university campuses also helps explain why all religious organizations are not a part of the sanctuary effort: "Campuses are ideologically and bureaucratically fraught geographies, and, counterintuitively, this makes them both ideal and inhospitable places for the [sanctuary] efforts" (159). Though there is so much potential for the US to live up to the promise of democracy, the exclusion of these ideals for noncitizens brings to light how immigration policy lacks idealism, often reconfiguring in response to political and economic demands.

My faith in the Sanctuary as a space for learning, despite the ideologically fraught tradition of religious organizations functioning as state apparatuses, came from the leadership and staff. Isabel was the main person I saw on the nights the English classes met from 6 to 8. Her job title was no doubt something like administrator or administrative assistant, but she did everything from making copies and coffee to serving as a floor cleaner, community organizer, and prayer leader. She could answer practical and logistical questions for teachers and students alike while carrying the emotional weight of uncertainties that befell the church. Isabel kept the day-to-day operations of not just the English program going, but the coordination of all of the church's community events. According to Isabel, members of the church and community said, "We need to learn English, and we need somewhere to learn English." Because the majority of volunteer teachers came through Matt, who everyone called "Mateo," we were trusted because they knew "what was in our hearts," as Mateo was fond of saying.

My teaching and research at the Sanctuary came about because Mateo was a friend of mine from my undergraduate study during the late 1990s at the University of California, Santa Barbara. After graduation in 2001, Mateo and I also taught elementary school for the calendar year of 2002 in Costa Rica. Mateo earned his MA in education after Costa Rica and taught for a few years in Mexico, before returning to the Bay Area to become a missionary in the Mission District of San Francisco. While I earned my PhD at the University of Arizona and researched the struggle to keep Mexican American ethnic studies courses as part of the curriculum in the Tucson Unified School District, Mateo was in charge at a halfway house where young men from Guatemala, Honduras, and other Latin American countries moved after having been released from juvenile detention. Many of them had been arrested for having sold drugs in the Tenderloin District of San Francisco. Mateo met these young men through his missionary outreach, having visited with youth locked in detention without any family or friends to come see them. Mateo told me, "A lot of them tell me that it [selling drugs] was the only work they could get because of their age and immigration statuses." While Mateo's missionary work follows a colonial tradition, his work with youth in the criminal justice system and

English language program attempts to offer help to those seeking it and who are often navigating these systems of exclusion and power.

For several years Mateo lived in the Mission District of San Francisco as the neighborhood was becoming gentrified. When I visited Mateo while he had the halfway house in the Mission District back in 2008, I walked with him up and down the streets as he stopped to speak in Spanish with older women and teenagers in the neighborhood. As a warning, Mateo told me, "At some point during the night, you'll probably hear an ambulance or maybe a police helicopter. Around the corner, there's a crack house and someone will call 9-1-1 because there's a lot of overdoses."

While serving as a missionary in the Mission District, Mateo would help the youth he met at the juvenile hall by offering missionary outreach and assistance finding legitimate work. Mateo often shared meals and led Bible study with them multiple times a week. He explained his faith-based work as such: "In the Bible, there are verses where God asks his followers to take care of strangers in their lands." He said this scripture often guided his work and that of other Christian organizations who work with immigrant populations. It seemed to hurt him on a spiritual level that politics got in the way of all religious organizations following this teaching. The radically local politics of property ownership became an issue at the Sanctuary when I was volunteering there, thereby bringing to bear the difficulty of a congregation trying to serve their community in spite of the racial bias written into the US legal system.

When I started teaching at the Sanctuary in 2013, Mateo had the English program going for about six months with a handful of volunteers who were often friends or acquaintances from local churches. With Mateo's background in education and his relationships with both local churches and English-speaking volunteers in the area, he and his missionary organization were a welcomed partnership with the Sanctuary church. Mateo and his wife Martha found volunteer teachers, scheduled days they could teach, and even taught in the early months of the program. The program grew from a single introductory class to an introductory class, two intermediate classes, and an advanced class, Monday through Wednesday.

While my role at the Sanctuary was as a teacher, the purpose of this book is not a pedagogical handbook for teaching English language learners or an administrative treatise for implementing and facilitating a community learning center (see Rachael Wendler Shah's *Rewriting Partnerships* or Ashley Holmes's *Public Pedagogy in Composition Studies* for discussions on community partnerships). This book ideally contributes some additional nuance and context to the ongoing conversation by immigration rhetoric scholars like

Christa Olson, Lisa A. Flores, Josue David Cisneros, and Karma Chávez. Their work highlights an immigration policy that discriminates and dehumanizes to deflect from the US legacy of neocolonial intervention. This book contributes decolonial methodology and critical race theory in the epistemological project of learning from migrant experiences about language and discrimination while imagining the possibility of other worlds. In addition, its exigent focus on the historical legacy of colonialism contextualizes and complicates the topos of immigration and the corresponding xenophobic category of "bad" migrant and "secure borders" rhetoric.

In the high-priced, exclusionary space of the Bay Area, the site of the Sanctuary stood in stark contrast as it was a space where migrants could come together with the goal of navigating the competing oppressive racial, linguistic, and citizenship matrices of colonial power. These kinds of community resources are becoming less available amidst the staggering economic inequality in the Bay Area, further exacerbated by the wealth of the Silicon Valley technology industry. I agree with Eithne Luibhéid's succinct summation that "the United States in recent years has facilitated the ever-expanding flow of capital, goods, information, and technology across borders—while at the same time cracking down on immigration, especially by the poor" (xviii). The Sanctuary offers a space in the Bay Area where migrants come to learn English so they can "participate in public discourse, to be perceived as fully literate" because these abilities serve as "a marker of citizenship and legitimacy" (Young 6). This book offers various scenes and a narration of my experiences at the Sanctuary that underscore the realities of how colonial legacies impact those displaced by US business and governmental interventions. While I never questioned the "legitimacy" of my students because of their English abilities or citizenship status, I recognize how US monolingual ideology permeates the everyday interactions of English language learners. Rhetorics of immigration scholars like Ana Ribero are correct in their description of "citizenship as performative" (*Dreamer* 11), so I remained critical of the promises of literacy that the English classes represented while prioritizing how I could be of service to the students as people. The Sanctuary was a more inclusive space than the workplaces, stores, hospitals, and schools where these adult students had to enter and experience overt or subtle forms of linguistic discrimination.

Guatemalan migrants in particular sought refuge in spaces like the Sanctuary church in the US because their home countries have been impacted by violence and displacement. In some cases, Indigenous Guatemalans have become the scapegoats for narco drug traffickers who benefit from governmental instability and corruption:

> In the Sierra del Lacandón National Park, on the border with Mexico, the
> eviction of an entire community of peasants gained national media atten-
> tion. The minister of interior, Carlos Menocal, accused the peasants of drug
> trafficking, and TV media seemed to be celebrating the displacement of 300
> families who were supposedly working for infamous narcos. (O. Martínez,
> *History* 64)

The Sanctuary is but one church near economic hubs like San Francisco and
the Silicon Valley where the experiences of these migrants come as a result
of US intervention and dependency on the drug trade and are representative
across other Latin American countries.

Prior to the current attention to migrant caravans from Central America,
previous waves of migrants came from Guatemala as refugees of the "civil
war," or the attempted genocides of Indigenous peoples. When I refer to the
"civil war" in this book, I often use "civil war" / *la violencia* like anthropologist Linda Green and others characterize the lasting impact of the "civil war"
violence, often referred to as simply *la violencia,* in many cases scorched-earth
campaigns by the Guatemalan military. Green explains:

> Present estimates account for more than 100,000 people killed and another
> 40,000 people disappeared in the course of one of the longest-running
> insurgencies in Latin America. During the 1980s alone, tens of thousands
> of refugees—men, women, and children—fled across the Mexican border,
> while another million people were internally displaced. (4)

Judith Zur cites GAM, a Guatemalan human rights organization, which
documented increases in violence in the last year of the "civil war" / *la violencia* from the year prior: "In 1996, GAM (1997) alone registered 69 political killings, seven massacres, the murder of 58 children, and 109 disappearances, an 11
percent increase on 1995" (5). This increase in violence at the end of the "civil
war" offers important historical context for this recent wave of migrants seeking refuge in the US due to gang and drug violence. Many in this more recent
wave of migrants were born during or shortly after this prolonged period of
human rights abuses. When Trump stoked the fear of his political base with
tweets about caravans and when Kamala Harris said "Do not come," they overlooked Guatemala's recent history and the current lack of governmental infrastructure and the trust of the Guatemalan people. This recent history set the
stage for the violence of gangs and the theft of land by narco-traffickers and
transnational corporations (O. Martínez, *History*; Torres; Ujpán).

In perhaps the most well-known writing about the Guatemalan "civil war" / *la violencia, I, Rigoberta Menchú*, Indigenous K'iche' human rights activist Rigoberta Menchú Tum gives her testimony about her family's and Indigenous community's struggles against the Guatemalan government and military. Menchú describes the violence inflicted by the government against the indigenous K'iche', whose lands were taken and people killed by the ethnically Ladino (European-heritage) government. I offer a content warning for Menchú's graphic description of the torture of her brother and a woman from a nearby village who had been accused of being communists and subversives:

> In my brother's case, he was cut in various places. His head was shaved and slashed. He had no nails. He had no soles to his feet. The earlier wounds were suppurating from infection. And the woman compañera, of course I recognized her; . . . They had shaved her private parts. The nipple of one of her breasts was missing and her other breast was cut off. . . . She was bitten all over, that compañera. She had no ears. (178)

Menchú's experience offers early concrete examples that help to explain why so many sought refuge from Guatemala during the country's thirty-six years of violence against Indigenous Maya. At the same time, the violence Menchú describes also gestures toward the gender-based violence against women that continues to the present, violence I discuss in greater detail in chapter 3.

I, Rigoberta was an important book for raising awareness about the atrocities of the genocide, a book that helped contribute to the official end of the "civil war." For Menchú's advocacy on behalf of Indigenous Guatemalans, she was awarded the Nobel Peace Prize in 1992. However, with the homicide rates in Guatemala remaining at almost the same levels following the end of the "civil war" (Taft-Morales), other Guatemalan Maya, though reverent of Menchú's work, disagree with the claims of peace she is said to have helped usher into Guatemala. In *Joseño: Another Mayan Voice Speaks from Guatemala*, Ignacio Bizarro Ujpán, a Tzutuhil Maya, comments, "It seems to me that she herself is deceptive by saying abroad that she has fought in order to obtain peace in Guatemala. It [peace] is a lie; we every day are exploited and marginalized, and the land that truly belongs to us Guatemalans is in the control of the millionaire" (20). Ujpán's criticism of Menchú's claim to peace is important for understanding migration from Guatemala and how narratives of peace only seem to benefit transnational business interests that continue to operate in spite of the high rates of violence. The homicide rate continued, but the narrative of peace supports the US responding with "zero tolerance" policies, separating families at the border, and the metaphorical wagging of a finger at would-be migrants like insolent children.

The epigraph of Mario Puzo's *The Godfather* is a quote attributed to Honoré de Balzac that states, "Behind every great fortune *is a great crime*" (Puzo 1; emphasis added). The high murder rates and violence in Central America have been attributed to drug traffickers who fight competing narcos and kill Indigenous campesinos as a part of the cost of doing business. Whether the US exported an ideology of free market capitalism, Latin America remains rhetorically interconnected, and the model of free market capitalism through violent robber barons was set. Journalist Óscar Martínez reports on the impact of the drug trade in Guatemala, pointing out that "ninety percent of the cocaine that arrives in the United States passes through Guatemala" (*History* 145). Though less direct than its backing of the Guatemalan government during the "civil war," the US continues to impact Latin American countries through the consumption of drugs and a capitalist demand that functions as a form of neocolonialism, or the exploitation of a country with less power. The extraction and exportation of natural resources parallel those of previous eras of colonialism, especially when the cost of these projects is the loss of Native lives. While some might argue that the drug trade is hardly Christopher Columbus cutting off the hands of Indigenous people who did not bring him enough gold, the displaced Central American youths forced to sell dope in the Tenderloin as disposable labor while overdoses happen like clockwork bear brutal similarities.

There is a need to decenter the focus of the conversation from the perspective of the US and decolonize the approach to thinking about the movement of people across space. In this book, the topoi of immigration and citizenship in the US are discussed with regard to the Indigenous Guatemalan Maya who have come to the US seeking opportunities and refuge from violence. As a deliberate decision, I use "migrant" for people leaving their countries, in much the same way Eithne Luibhéid explains the term as referring "to anyone who has crossed an international border to reach the United States," making "no distinction among legal immigrants, refugees, asylum seekers, or undocumented immigrants" (xi). I use the term "immigration" to discuss the rhetoric and policy around the enforcement of bodies moving across space. I choose to do so because as rhetorician Johanna Hartelius writes in *The Rhetorics of US Immigration: Identity, Community, Otherness,* naming plays an important role in how the subjects of the discussion are portrayed: "Of primary concern to rhetoricians has long been the problematic representation of immigrants in official discourses and mass media" (3). Similarly, Lisa A. Flores argues in *Deportable and Disposable: Public Rhetoric and the Making of the "Illegal"*

Immigrant that certain racialized terms have come to mischaracterize Mexicans, and by default all Latin Americans, as illegal: "Frequent and persistent characterizations of Mexican migrants as temporary, cheap labor have, in effect, constructed in the cultural imaginary an image of Mexicans as deportable and disposable and racialized them into 'illegality'" (4). In an effort to avoid some of the more problematic terms, in this book the use of "migrant" is a strategic sidestepping of the term "immigrant," which is often politicized and coupled with the rhetoric of illegality undergirding exclusion from citizenship.

Because the ecology of topics related to the Sanctuary includes immigration, citizenship, race, ethnicity, and language, critical race theory provides a prescient framework that identifies inherent racial biases within the legal system that impacts this ecology. CRT stems from the work of legal scholar Derrick Bell, who as far back as 1976 noted in the *Yale Law Journal* that the subjectivity of the law, with regard to how it was disproportionately enforced against people of color, reinforced racial discrimination like segregation in schools ("Serving"). Legal precedence and rhetoric were intertwined, affecting people of color through the intentional targeting of populations of color by laws relating to aspects such as citizenship: African Americans in slavery counted as three-fifths of a person for representation and tax purposes; Jim Crow laws enforced a second-class citizenship of freed African Americans; and contemporary over-policing of Blacks and Latinos feeds the prison industrial complex (Alexander). CRT legal scholar Cheryl Harris's description of whiteness as property that conferred citizenship rights articulates an important intersection that helps explain how and why exclusion functions: "Whiteness conferred on its owners aspects of citizenship that were all the more valued because they were denied to others. Indeed, the very fact of citizenship itself was linked to white racial identity" (1744). In rhetoric and composition studies, Aja Martinez helped usher in the CRT methodology of counterstory as a framework for speaking back and resisting dominant "majoritarian" and "stock" stories normalizing and perpetuating white supremacy. In this book, counterstory provides a methodology for responding to somewhat typical assumptions a well-meaning white volunteer teacher at the Sanctuary expressed about the lack of goals her students had for learning English. The stock stories of Black, Indigenous, and people of color (BIPOC) students and families "caring less" about education speaks to CRT's first tenet, about the permanence of racism in US society, which allows for these narratives to circulate, despite the reality of structural obstacles BIPOC communities have that are not always considered.

For the Indigenous migrant students at the Sanctuary, English literacy is regarded, if not as a stepping stone toward US citizenship, then at least as a step toward social mobility at their job or an aspirational new job that is a part of the promise of a better life in the US. Morris Young explains that the acquisition of literacy is seemingly more complicated because the "perception of a person's citizenship is overdetermined because of competing ideological constructions about literacy and race" (7). Racism is something many Indigenous Guatemalans experienced as a part of the rationale for the attempted genocide or "civil war." Even when discussing the topic of the Spanish language, Menchú's translator makes the point that Menchú learned Spanish for survival against the neocolonial genocide by the Guatemalan government. Menchú's translator explains in the book's introduction that "words are her only weapons" (xi). Describing Menchú's relationship with the colonial language of Spanish, her translator writes that "Spanish was a language which was forced upon her" (xii). Critical literacy scholars like Gabriela Ríos support the resistance of Indigenous folks to learning colonial languages when Ríos questions literacy as a goal for Indigenous populations. Ríos argues that Indigenous land-based literacies that constitute an aspect of their knowledge-traditions are minimized and not acknowledged or honored as enough.

Decolonial theory and frameworks centering Indigenous land and knowledge provide important practices for understanding how earlier and recent waves of migrant caravans have their origins in the land displacement of settler colonialism. In "Settler Colonialism and the Elimination of the Native," Patrick Wolfe describes the desire for land as the central focus of settler colonialism: "Whatever settlers may say . . . the primary motive for elimination is not race (or religion, ethnicity, grade of civilization, etc.) but access to territory. Territoriality is settler colonialism's specific, irreducible element" (388). Even before the genocide of the Maya in Guatemala during the "civil war" (Sanford), the government worked with US companies to expatriate the majority of agriculturally rich land from Indigenous communities for corporate farming (Torres; Ujpán). As an outgrowth of neocolonialism that centers business interests, the capitalist goal of acquiring this land, commodified as "real estate," follows the foundational prioritizing of product and profits over the people who worked to cultivate this land. Scholars of Indigenous studies remind us how land gives life through food, but also educates and instills knowledge in the people who care for it (Green; Mukavetz; Ríos). While Wolfe's definition of settler colonialism prioritizes access to territory, the knowledge traditions of the space remain central to building decolonial epistemology and to understanding the layers of trauma enacted through displacement.

The topic of land became more of a local issue to the Indigenous migrant student population at the Sanctuary because of a struggle over the Sanctuary's lease with a predominantly white congregation who shared the property. Though land is central to the approach of many Indigenous rhetorical scholars, Walter Mignolo approaches decoloniality through the identification of the phenomenon of modernity as a driving force of colonialism (*Darker*). Still, in Wolfe's discussion of the link between settler colonialism and genocide, he concedes, in contrast to Mignolo, that "modernity cannot explain the insatiable dynamic whereby settler colonialism always needs more land" (395). Recognizing how the taking of resources serves as a motive of colonialism, neocolonialism, and settler colonialism, we can see how the goal of profit helps to account for the project of gentrification. Neocolonialism is explicitly linked to capitalism, whereas traditional colonialism might be thought of more as the expansion of imperial power through religion, language, and inscribing cultural hierarchies, so settler colonialism represents the occupation of land and the assumption of authority over this stolen land. In the East Bay, as in many urban locations across the US targeted for development, gentrification embodies the insatiable consumption of land as property for the purpose of renovation and flipping or leasing at higher rates.

At the Sanctuary, the adult migrant students are confronted by their lack of power as noncitizens when trying to work with the predominantly white, English-speaking congregation who is the same Christian denomination and shares the lease with their own church on the same plot of land. This shared piece of property became a source of contention when the predominantly white, English-speaking church leadership re-signed the lease on the property without the Latinx, Spanish-speaking Sanctuary church who had previously been cosigners of the lease. In doing so, the English-speaking church used language and citizenship against the nonwhite congregation at the Sanctuary, which follows in line with the displacement of settler colonialism. The lack of power of the Sanctuary church demonstrates what CRT scholar Derrick Bell said about the laws in the US being written for the protection of property for white citizens ("Brown . . . Forty-Five Years" 176). In *An Afro-Indigenous History of the United States,* Kyle T. Mays reiterates this point: "One could become a property owner through enslavement and Indigenous dispossession, both of which contributed to the development of white citizenship" (19). The criminalization and over-policing of undocumented migrants can therefore be seen as a direct manifestation from white panic about property as the logical outcome of undocumented migrants "stealing jobs." This logic of criminalization is defined by scarcity in response to an insatiable desire for territory that tragically continues in a tradition of displacing Indigenous peoples, even as they migrate, having already been victimized by expropriation.

WHAT THIS BOOK DOES

In addition to following rhetorician Olson's assertion to keep an eye on Latin America in our examinations of US rhetoric, this book contributes to a larger call within the field of writing and rhetorical studies. This call seeks to incorporate critical methodologies for accurately communicating the experiences and perspectives of BIPOC communities when it comes to issues of inequality such as race, class, sexuality, gender, and disability (Cedillo; Haas; A. Martinez "American Way," *Counterstory,* and "Critical Race Theory"; Perryman-Clark; Pimentel; Ore; Ruiz). Teaching students "at risk" is a familiar trope of education research, but less attention has been paid to the matrices of factors impacting students fleeing violence in their home countries and experiencing dehumanizing rhetorics and policies in the US.

The discrimination these adult Indigenous students faced both at home and in the US provokes the application of decolonial and critical race frameworks to examine what happens within and outside of the US border. To make meaning from observations, surveys, and interviews necessitates a deliberate process of ethical consideration with regard to how information about this vulnerable population would be shared. Decolonial methodologies differ from traditional research, as Godwin Agboka notes, where researchers often already have their argument that they are collecting data to confirm: "In many cases, these studies were designed even before the researchers arrived at the research sites, reflecting the unreflexive and predictable posture of these studies and their research questions" (301). At the Sanctuary, some of my questions about race or violence were discussed and regarded with a learned vagueness or silence as a result of the history of genocide and a tradition of displacement that institutionalizes and internalizes both fear and racism. The decision of many migrants to remain silent can be a deliberate strategy of language negotiation. As these migrant students learn English, Laura Gonzales reminds us that in translation, experiences with power continue to inform these negotiations. She adds that being a translator "requires translators to live and relive instances of communicative negotiation, making decisions in the moment based on our previous experiences with language, power, and marginalization" (7). It was never my goal as a teacher or researcher for my students to relive their histories of violence during class or in our informal conversations before and after class. However, these legacies are often already part of the experiences they relive as multilingual speakers negotiating languages.

This book asks readers to consider a rhetorical examination of race, citizenship, and language through a mixed-method approach with both critical race theory and decolonial theory. These theories underpin the ethnographic methods that communicate the perspectives of migrants through interviews, surveys, and participant observation. Although my personal narrative, experiences, culture, and beliefs shape this research, I use the survey and narrative data as heuristics for the purpose of working out the knotted ecologies of decolonial knowledge and the lived experiences of BIPOC communities. Decolonial and CRT scholars readily acknowledge that an observer's choices about what to note and which questions to ask are just as subjective as the hermeneutic process the empirical researcher undertakes in the presentation of what audiences are to understand as "fact." The selected narrative elements included at the beginning and end, and sometimes interspersed through most chapters, follow the use of storytelling in Indigenous decolonial practices as well as critical race theory methods that value lived experience for knowledge-making.

The theoretical and methodological approach of CRT recognizes the permanence of the kind of jingoistic, white supremacist ideology that became more overt during Trump's presidential campaign during the latter part of my time at the Sanctuary. With its origins in legal studies, CRT reveals how BIPOC communities are disproportionately impacted by policy dating back to the US Constitution, which categorized nonwhite, noncitizens as chattel property (Bell, "Brown . . . Forty-Five Years"; Harris; Ore). When Trump took office, racist ideology became reified into policy such as the "zero tolerance" policy that served to concretize the dehumanization of nonwhite noncitizens. Immigration scholars have advocated for the application of CRT to studies of this sociological phenomenon because the issue of race and ethnicity is indistinguishable from political discourse and policy. The manifestation of this discourse into policy, more often than not, disadvantages nonwhites in a US immigration and legal system where few asylum cases are successful and the number of unskilled labor visas is but a fraction of the number of those attempting to enter the US.

Although the Sanctuary church and English program serve predominantly Indigenous Latinx students, the struggle the Spanish-speaking Sanctuary church has with the English-speaking church sharing the same property raises important questions about how these programs can come under attack in radically local contexts. Research at sites like the Sanctuary has been advocated for by Latinx critical race (LatCrit) scholars like Laura Chávez-Moreno, who argues that spaces where Latinx students learn English contribute to how we might understand racism operating in other bilingual education contexts: "How these bilingual education spaces address anti-Latinx racism and white supremacy could offer different insights into the challenges they face and lessons they may offer other contexts" (113). For LatCrit scholars, topics like immigration, language, and education remain important issues because of the interconnectedness of these issues and what the policies impacting them reveal.

Race, language, citizenship, and property have all been impacted by the enduring legacies of racism in the US and colonial legacies in the US and Central America. English language education scholar Tonda Liggett applies critical race theory to how English language learners are impacted by racism, as evidenced through linguicism, or discrimination based on language use. Liggett explains that

> the first aspect is to explore the notion of linguicism as an ordinary, permanent fixture in society. This would entail examining how ELLs [English language learners] routinely encounter discrimination based on language proficiency and accent in their school community and beyond. The second aspect would be to analyze the historic effects of European colonialism. (121)

Attention to European colonialism underscores important concerns about the role of teaching English—or Spanish, for that matter—to Indigenous populations as a promise of social mobility through literacy, or simply another instantiation of settler colonialism. The maintenance of Indigenous languages has been identified and explored as a decolonial practice educators of rhetoric should be concerned with and incorporate into the classroom. Rhetoric scholar Qwo-Li Driskill explains that "Indigenous languages not only carry cultural memory, because language is so central to rhetoric, they also change the way we think about rhetoric and how rhetoric works" (67). So many continue to resist changing how we think about language and rhetoric because of the pervasive nature of monolingual ideology, not just in the US but within the field of writing studies, and because so many remain direct beneficiaries of its exclusionary worldview.

As I noted in the beginning of this introduction, the moments at the church English program captured in this book occurred during the three-year period spanning from about September of 2013 to May of 2016. During this time, I taught English as a second language (ESL) as a volunteer for a community-based program operated out of a Spanish-speaking church I call the Sanctuary in the East Bay. Based on observations during teaching and stories that came from interviews, I somewhat naively sought to answer questions such as, To what extent does the English language provide access to the American Dream? Do the students believe in the American Dream, or do they simply desire a better life free of violence? How do they perceive or experience discrimination as racially marked migrants? While the "American Dream" has been demystified from within the US, I wondered to what extent this myth circulated among those who had recently crossed over and in spite of the realities of anti-Latinx legislation. Senate Bill 1070, which had passed in states like Arizona, for instance, authorized all police to act as immigration enforcement. What I found myself confronted with was the economy of exclusion that affects immigration policy in the US and how gentrification continues to impact populations already displaced by the free market forces of drug trafficking. In many ways, I learned from the culture of silence many of them learned as a strategy to protect against the high rates of crime, homicide, and gender-based violence in their home countries. Languaging with these vulnerable populations highlights how language serves as a barrier for inclusion that is written into education policy. The struggle of the Sanctuary's staff and congregation over their lease agreement during my time there illuminated enduring racial hierarchies institutionalized through laws regarding citizenship and property in the US.

This book contributes to the humanizing efforts of research on migrant populations stripped of human rights, especially in relation to the recent history of anti-immigrant policy such as Trump's "zero tolerance" immigration policy. This policy even had stock speculation outlet Market Watch recommending investment in private prisons (Toy). As rhetorician Olson advocated, we can hardly think about the rhetoric of secure borders and criminalizing migrants without an eye to Latin America due in a large part to the interrelatedness among these rhetorical ecologies. When those in power appeal to the fear of their political audiences, their purpose is to gain support of dehumanizing policies rather than address the reasons so many Central Americans risk their lives and safety against robbery, kidnapping, and sexual violence to seek refuge in the US (Arellano; Rizzo). This book enacts decolonial practices that seek to redress the impacts of (neo)colonialism on Indigenous Guatemalans who migrate, having been pushed off of their traditional farmlands by weak governments corrupted by the wealth of narco drug traffickers and transnational corporations (O. Martínez, *History*). Research as a part of individual and collaborative community efforts like the work of the Sanctuary serves to take action against the void of inhumanity enacted through immigration policy.

Much of the narrative in this book is based on ethnographic participant observation and interviews that provoke more questions than the descriptions and quotes answer. Many interactions in the following chapters serve as provocations to untangle the United States' complicit role in the neocolonial attempts at genocide in countries like Guatemala. They also show how these legacies impact current immigration from Latin American countries with similar histories of US intervention. Each chapter seeks to unravel an aspect related to the larger topic of immigration. I apply CRT and decolonial theory to make sense of the exclusion of citizenship, histories of past and present-day violence in Central America, property and land displacement, linguistic difference, and literacy myths that hurt Indigenous populations. Based on volunteer experiences, this book similarly helps show how much we might not know about the histories, fear, and pain of neighbors, employees, coworkers, and friends we are interconnected with.

SUMMARY OF CHAPTERS

Chapter 1 begins with a migrant student from Guatemala, Antonio, questioning the limitations of English education and research. His question prompts exploration into California's legacy of exclusionary immigration policy and the colonial legacy privileging economic growth that impacts violence in Central America. When elected pope in 2013, Pope Francis shared his beliefs about what he calls an economy of exclusion in *Evangelii gaudium* (*The Joy of the Gospel*), where he decries an economy that exploits and throws away people. Pope Francis's argument provides a guiding concept for understanding the motivations of the predominantly Indigenous migrants from Guatemala at the Sanctuary who seek refuge while continuing to experience marginalization. While many come to the US for safety, migrants experience a climate of criminalization that targets communities of color and upholds economic and racial exclusion. These immigration policies maintain exclusion from citizenship for nonwhites that has benefitted white citizens since the 1848 Treaty of Guadalupe-Hidalgo, when California became a US territory. This strategy has continued all the way to the present day, with the manipulation of H-1B visas by tech companies to exploit skilled, noncitizen labor. H-1B visas allow companies to pay noncitizens less than their US counterparts, while many times keeping H-1B visa holders offshore. Critical race theory serves as a necessary lens for understanding how citizenship laws in the US were created for the protection of the property of white citizens. The economy of exclusion also raises questions that decolonial theory addresses, specifically how Indigenous Guatemalans have been displaced from their land because of violence resulting from settler colonial capitalism.

In chapter 2, I outline the tenets of decolonial critical race theory to explain how white supremacist policy impacts US and transnational Indigenous populations who are forced to migrate due to neocolonial capitalism. This chapter enacts a grounded theory by bringing decolonial theory and CRT together to "develop new concepts, often linking many ideas not previously connected across the many research silos that make up the field" (Martin et al. 13). This chapter builds on the pluriversal possibilities of CRT and decolonial theory, which Ali Meghji articulates in "Towards a Theoretical Synergy: Critical Race Theory and Decolonial Thought in Trumpamerica and Brexit Britain." A grounded theory of decolonial critical race theory helps articulate connections between racism on a local political level and colonial projects on a transnational scale, as in Meghji's critique: "Trump's campaign, therefore, was not only committed to giving back valuation to white citizens who felt marginalized in their own country (as CRT shows), but also giving valuation back to the nation on a global scale (which decolonial thought can show)" (9). Trump's campaign rhetoric intensified toward the end of my time at the Sanctuary, and the decolonial CRT tenets respond to these intersecting issues of race/ethnicity, immigration, language, and land that provoke the exigency for the Sanctuary as a space and concept bringing together these aligning theories. The issues within and outside the US affect the predominantly Indigenous Guatemalan student population at the Sanctuary, as do many Indigenous populations living through the lasting effects of colonialism, neocolonialism, and settler colonialism. Chapter 2 additionally outlines the methods and methodologies I used, as I outline ethnographic tools and instruments as well as the explanation I incorporated for the guiding concepts to interpret the data and findings.

Chapter 3 explores the topic of violence as a motivation for many migrants to make the dangerous journey to the US. When surveyed about reasons the adult migrant students at the Sanctuary came to the US, many cited work opportunities, others cited violence in their home country, and others preferred not to answer. These responses spoke to the culture of silence many Indigenous Maya have learned from having grown up in or having had close family members who survived the attempted genocide of Indigenous people, or the "civil war." The recent history of the government's forced conscription of young Maya into the military during the "civil war" included a campaign of scorched earth on other Indigenous villages that can hardly be ignored in terms of the generational trauma. The Indigenous men and women suspected of being subversives were tortured and disappeared, further contributing to distrust within communities and the rupturing of the social fabric of many Maya communities in Guatemala. In recent years more and more women have risked crossing over to the US, knowing the high rates of sexual assault because femicide and gender-based violence have increased in Central America (Obinna). Because femicide along the US border has widely been regarded as a cost of transnational business, decolonial theory provides a framework for identifying the violence of capitalism in neocolonialism.

Chapter 4 begins with the uncertain future of the Sanctuary because of a struggle over the property's lease. The predominantly white, English-speaking congregation sharing the property with the Spanish-speaking Sanctuary church signed the lease for the shared property without including the Sanctuary. The Sanctuary's pastor, staff, and congregation feared eviction without their inclusion on the lease following unproductive talks that demonstrated a perceived lack of a genuine desire to resolve the issue on the part of the English-speaking leadership. The Sanctuary church's dispute with the English-speaking congregation about the lease provokes important questions about how linguistic and racial differences support property ownership and citizenship. The lack of communication between the two congregations is further complicated by the language difference that positions the Spanish-speaking Sanctuary staff at a disadvantage. Little is done by the English-speaking congregation or the church's governing body to accommodate language differences in order to settle the issue. Chapter 4 further examines the issue of language through survey data and through interview responses that reveal how many of the students share the Indigenous Mayan language of Mam. Poignantly, the struggle over the Sanctuary serves a metonymy for the issue of gentrification across the East Bay, as economic interests undermine the role of the Sanctuary church in the community and threaten to displace this community yet again.

Chapter 5 draws on the critical race theory methodology of counterstory in an examination and response to dominant narratives about immigrant laborers and education, including access and the honoring of land-based knowledge. In CRT counterstory, the majoritarian stock story communicates assumptions and beliefs in the prevailing narrative, which is represented by the sentiments of a volunteer teacher who is frustrated because she continues to have the same students in her advanced class. Student perspectives provide an important counterstory for responding to these dominant narratives that more often than not portray the migrant students as not caring about learning English or even not caring about education in general. Decolonial approaches to understanding Indigenous knowledge and relationships with land help address stock stories that critical literacy scholar Gabriela Ríos describes as the myth of literacy acquisition. The stock story of immigrants coming to the US for a better life is complicated by the widespread violence in Guatemala by gangs and drug traffickers that causes many Indigenous Guatemalans to seek refuge.

Chapter 6 provides some resolution for some of the questions raised in this chapter and across the chapters that follow. It seems fitting to conclude with a chapter related to teaching because this book shines a light on some of the professional shadows that cloud our journeys as scholar-teachers; yet, the concluding chapter provides some resolutions, complications, and further questions about the role of literacy and the limitations imposed by policy unrelated to education. What presidential campaigns and administrations can in fact teach is that US history benefits from education being replaced by nationalistic belief in the United States' continued exceptionalism and mythical greatness. The moments of people's lives I capture in the following pages testify to the dreams of migrants who seek refuge in hopes of making better lives for themselves and their families because these hopes are the best chances for making the United States the place of dreams realized.

CHAPTER 1

Citizenship, Economies of Exclusion, and Tech Money

HOW CAN YOU HELP ME?

One night while I was volunteer-teaching at the Sanctuary, during the fifteen-minute break between the 6 to 8 p.m. class, one of my students in the intermediate class, Antonio, questioned in Spanish what I might accomplish with my research. I had been volunteering as an English language teacher at the Sanctuary's program for over a year when I first asked the adult migrant students if they would fill out anonymous surveys to help with my *investigaciones académicas* (academic research). The news at the time was giving airtime to businessman Trump, who had taken up the "birther" conspiracy accusing the first Black president, Barack Obama, of having a fake birth certificate, thereby contributing to the mainstream circulation of white nationalist ideology into the national dialogue.

Antonio was a man in his early twenties with relatively light skin and longish, slicked-back hair. He said, "I'm a guest in this country. How can you help me?" He stared at me, restating the question with the same serious expression. Other students sitting at the same table looked on, curious about our exchange. When one of the other students reexplained what I had said about being interested in perceptions of language, Antonio waved off the explanation. He nodded to indicate that he had understood what I hoped to learn. The rationale I used on Internal Review Board (IRB) applications did not interest

24

him. He seemed to be asking what the purpose of volunteers teaching English and conducting research was if there was little I could offer to help him in the US, which was, by default, *my* country. His question made the haunting limitations of my volunteering and researching come out from the shadows.

The other male students, many of them Indigenous Maya I had taught for the past year, waved their hands at Antonio, motioning for him to relax. It was an uncomfortable moment. It was unlike any of the other exchanges I experienced with the other adult students during my three years teaching at the Spanish-speaking church's English program. During most breaks, students would sometimes want to practice speaking English with me by asking me about myself, asking questions about English, or using simple phrases we had covered. The repetition of Antonio's question in Spanish seemed to go beyond problematizing the reciprocity of providing information decolonial scholars like Linda Tuhiwai Smith address and seemed to raise the question of what ends this information would achieve. In class Antonio could sometimes seem more confrontational than any of the other students because he was less willing in classroom exercises to play along in dialogues. At one point he said he washed dishes, but in later conversations he said he was looking for work. I understood that his frustration may not have even entirely been related to our discussion, although maybe it was still related to the unfulfilled promise of a better life that the acquisition of English literacy suggested. Or had other past life experiences robbed him of the ability to be playful?

While conducting research in Guatemala for *Fear as a Way of Life: Mayan Widows in Rural Guatemala,* Linda Green explains she similarly experienced Maya agreeing to speak with her before rescinding with questions similar to those I experienced: "Others asked me directly how their association with this academic project might benefit them" (21). Green explains that the Guatemalan military created levels of distrust within communities that affected all levels of social interaction: "The Guatemalan military's strategy of using Mayan boys as foot soldiers in the counterinsurgency war and using local men as civil patrollers . . . to carry out surveillance on their neighbors and at times to commit murder has led to severe ruptures in family and community social relations" (31). A culture of learned distrust would be a good reason for Antonio to question anyone in a position of authority. The context of the Sanctuary church provided a kind of safe space where he might have felt more comfortable voicing his frustrations.

Like many students at the Sanctuary classes, Antonio came from Guatemala, a Central American country that is often overlooked in political and educational contexts. Many of the adult students at the Spanish-speaking Sanctuary church are Indigenous Maya from Guatemala. They are the very same people fleeing violence in Central America, much like the caravans of migrants traveling together through Mexico that President Trump vilified while in office. According to Salvador Rizzo of the *Washington Post,* Trump was quoted as telling reporters: "Go into the middle of the caravan, take your cameras and search. Okay? Search. . . . You're going to find MS-13, you're going to find Middle Eastern, you're going to find everything." Making threats about gangs and potential terrorists, Trump mischaracterized the caravans as though they were a singular, monolithic threat rather than vulnerable people traveling in groups for protection. Rizzo fact-checked these remarks and reported that Trump's administration "provided no evidence" to substantiate the fear spread about migrants. The Associated Press explains that one of the caravans was made up of

> more than 1,600 [people] by the time it reached the Guatemalan border, fueled by word of mouth and media coverage even as US President Donald Trump tweeted criticism of the caravan. Migrants have increasingly banded together to travel through Mexico, believing the dangerous journey is safer to make in large numbers. Dozens of Central American migrants have been kidnapped by gangs demanding money or shaken down by police. Some have been killed along the way. ("AP Explains")

At the Sanctuary, the world of politics seemed to elicit a shrug, as though all of that was well beyond what the students hoped to accomplish during their day-to-day affairs. The dangers of migrating are alluded to in the prayer requests that occur before the beginning of Monday night classes. Most of these requests are for a brother or sister, or a child they have not heard from.

Antonio's question also rings of pain and reminds me of the point rhetoric scholar José Cortez makes after volunteering with women and children migrating. Cortez explains how he understands why his own father never explained why he chose to migrate from Mexico. Additionally, he decides he would never ask any of the people he offered aid to for their reasons. My questions and surveys might not have triggered Antonio's confrontation, but the fact is that many US citizens tend to be unaware that "following the official end of the 36-year armed conflict in 1996, violence in Guatemala has transformed from political, to more widespread social and economic violence" (Winton, "Youth" 170). Antonio's question rings with almost the accusation of "How could you not know?" or "Why does no one seem to care?"

This chapter touches on the tradition of citizenship and the construction of the white citizen through policies positioning nonwhites as foreigners so as to protect property meant for white citizenship and illustrates how these practices continue through the manipulation of H-1B visas in the Silicon Valley. Josue Cisneros's definition of citizenship in *The Border Crossed Us: Rhetorics of Borders, Citizenship, and Latina/o Identity* provides a useful way for interpreting the rhetorical nature of citizenship in relation to inclusion and exclusion: "As an 'imaginary,' citizenship entails legal and institutional as well as figurative and cultural dimensions; citizenship indexes legal status and political rights but also refers to one's inclusion in a sociocultural and 'imagined' community" (5). In the Bay Area of Northern California, the Silicon Valley tech money continues the tradition of churning through nonwhite labor outside of the "imagined community" in ways traced back to California's gold rush and the Indigenous Ohlone and Muwekma contact with Spanish missionaries. In Pope Francis's terms, Silicon Valley tech wealth further perpetuates an economy that relies on migrants for cheap labor while hiding behind laws regarding citizenship to exclude this population when there are any ethical concerns about companies paying "nonskilled" labor a living wage.

The Sanctuary church is located in the East Bay of Northern California. The Bay Area in Northern California can be inclusively defined as the South Bay cities within Silicon Valley, the peninsula with Palo Alto and the campuses of Facebook and Google along the way to San Francisco, and the East Bay and Oakland, Berkeley, and Alameda across the bridge. My university colleagues with experience in the tech industry will report that California legislators wait to finalize the state's budget until Silicon Valley companies report their yearly earnings as the tax dollars are that impactful. All of this occurs on land stolen from the Muwekma Ohlone tribes through congressional erasure and their false extinction validated by an academic researcher from UC Berkeley (Nijmeh). In this chapter I argue that the legacy of California policy regarding citizenship follows exclusionary beliefs about nonwhite citizens, which I analyze through a critical race theory lens to reveal the protection of white property.

ECONOMIES OF EXCLUSION

As I write about exclusion in the Bay Area in my office on a Jesuit campus where sections of a Catholic mission still stand, I find it difficult to disconnect some of the Judeo-Christian beliefs opposed to exclusion. Because the Sanctuary English program is based out of a church and Mateo, my college friend and English program coordinator, works as a missionary, I have also come to understand how Mateo and the Sanctuary leadership's belief systems informed their work, in spite of religion's role in colonial projects. Mateo explained to me that his Christian organization, which offers support for undocumented migrants, often cites biblical verses from Leviticus 19:33–34 where God tells his followers to support travelers and offer them aid in much the same way they were given assistance: "When a stranger sojourns with you in your land, you shall not do him wrong. You shall treat the stranger who sojourns with you as the native among you, and you shall love him as yourself, for you were strangers in the land of Egypt: I am the Lord your God." In many ways these biblical verses capture the spirit of liberatory Catholics who advocated for the Indigenous peoples in Guatemala during and after the thirty-six-year "civil war," or *la violencia*. Bishop Juan Gerardi Conedera was murdered for trying to bring justice for the many dead and disappeared during the scorched-earth military campaigns: "In April 1998, however, Bishop Juan Gerardi Conedera, working on behalf of the Catholic Church . . . released a report titled *Guatemala: nunca más* (*Guatemala: Never Again*), which blamed 80 percent of the killings on governmental forces. . . . Less than two days after he released the report, he was assassinated at his residence in Guatemala City" (Ujpán 10). The percentage of deaths attributed to the Guatemalan government is important, and I will return to this discussion later. At the same time, after talking with Mateo about the potential interpretation of the Bible with regard to immigration, Antonio's question is not without religious context and a history of activism.

In 2013 when I began both working at my Jesuit university and volunteering at the Sanctuary's English program, Pope Francis became head of the Catholic Church and began garnering attention for advocating for social justice. Before becoming the current leader of the Catholic Church, Pope Francis (born Jorge Mario Bergoglio) was a Jesuit in Buenos Aires, Argentina, which no doubt informed his advocacy for the poor and criticism of consumerism. In his writing and public commentary, Pope Francis criticizes free markets as exclusionary, violent, and oppressive. In his apostolic exhortation *Evangelii Gaudium (The Joy of the Gospel),* Pope Francis writes:

> Today we also have to say "thou shalt not" to an economy of exclusion and inequality. Such an economy kills. . . . Today everything comes under the laws of competition and the survival of the fittest, where the powerful feed upon the powerless. As a consequence, masses of people find themselves excluded and marginalized: without work, without possibilities, without any means of escape. Human beings are themselves considered consumer goods to be used and then discarded. We have created a "throwaway" culture which is now spreading. It is no longer simply about exploitation and oppression, but something new. . . . The excluded are not the "exploited" but the outcast, the "leftovers." (43)

This economy of exclusion that victimizes large populations in Guatemala, Honduras, and El Salvador operates for the US through a reactionary immigration system that often discriminates against those victimized elsewhere. At the same time, Pope Francis's advocacy for those "thrown away" calls attention to a tradition of social justice that has not always been explicit in the Catholic Church. Rhetoric scholar Anne Teresa Demo identifies earlier advocacy for those "thrown away" in a 2003 collaborative pastoral letter by the United States Conference of Catholic Bishops and the Conferencia del Episcopado Mexicano that reframes migrant advocacy. Demo explains that in the letter, *Strangers No Longer*, "the theological conversation about migration led by the Catholic Church actively employed a moral framework that recontextualized the debate over immigration enforcement and reframed the relative rights of migrants and sovereign states in politically significant ways" (50). In the case of the adult students at the Sanctuary, many of them could be considered part of the "exploited." Their experiences with immigration would benefit from a moral reframing in civic deliberations about what is often a politically partisan topic.

The "throwaway" culture Pope Francis describes applies to the predominantly Indigenous Guatemalan student population at the Sanctuary because many of them were displaced from post–"civil war" violence, transnational corporations, or drug trafficking. In *A History of Violence: Living and Dying in Central America*, journalist Óscar Martínez captures a snapshot of this widespread displacement in the municipality of Sayaxché. Martínez explains, "According to the National Council of Protected Areas, by 2007, close to 8,000 people have been displaced from 902 *caballerías* in and around the municipality of Sayaxché. Twenty-seven campesino communities ceded their land to African palm companies and other buyers" (72). With each "caballería" equaling about 110 acres, large swaths of traditional farming land for Indigenous populations were forcefully purchased or taken, leaving the Indigenous landowner without options. In an interview with an activist working with the Indigenous in Guatemala, Martínez finds there is often little difference between land being purchased and people being forced out:

> If the lawyer of a company visits you time and again and talks to you about five-figure numbers, and you're a Q'eqchi' campesino, your eyes start glowing and then you sell without knowing a thing. If you're a campesino, indigenous or otherwise, and the narcos want your land, then you're even more fucked, because they'll simply tell that you need to sell your land for such and such a price, and that's it. . . . There used to be a famous saying about a decade ago: If you don't sell now, your widow's gonna sell herself for cheap later. (66)

While some might resist Pope Francis's criticism of economies of exclusion, the ways in which Indigenous Guatemalans are displaced from their land in Martínez's account could only be described as cast off, thrown away, and exploited, as Pope Francis writes. Unfortunately, US politicians use the violence inflicted on Central Americans by drug traffickers as a reason to exclude them: "By creating the need to exclude based on threat, US citizenship could be reified through heightened fear of Latinx immigrants" (Wingard 50). US citizenship then excludes through the vilification of Latin American migrants who have already been marginalized.

Pope Francis's critique of an economy that excludes can further be seen in the gentrification of the Bay Area, where the economic divide has grown significantly in the past decade. In 2014 Andrew S. Ross, a journalist for the *San Francisco Gate,* reported that the "great divide in Silicon Valley's wealth grows even wider . . . [as] those making $100,000 and up, a group that constitutes 45 percent of the region's population, saw their incomes rise. Those making $35,000 to $99,000 (35 percent), or less than $35,000 (20 percent) saw their incomes fall." The immigrant student population at the Sanctuary makes up groups who saw their incomes fall, adding to the stress of being criminalized for seeking refuge. Pope Francis's critique of a free market economy could very well be informed by living in proximity to Latin American economies like Guatemala's, where the stark economic inequality can be seen as bolstering the lack of faith in governmental institutions. As Green explains, "Guatemala has one of the most unequal systems of land distribution in all of Latin America[:] 2 percent of the population owns between 65 and 70 percent of the arable land" (16). In the Bay Area, real estate prices rank among the highest in the US, and the Muwekma Ohlone Tribe continues its forty-year fight for governmental recognition; however, in Guatemala, land intersects with violence as oppression moves from the military's reign of terror against the Maya to the violence meted out by transnational corporations and narco-trafficking interests.

DECOLONIZING CALIFORNIA
IMMIGRATION POLICY WITH CRT

Pope Francis's criticism of economies that exclude provokes important questions about injustice that can be more closely considered through a racial lens. Rhetoric and critical race scholars have argued for the necessity of factoring race into discussions of citizenship and immigration because whiteness is often the overriding criteria for inclusion. While Pope Francis focuses on free markets in his criticism, it is impossible to disconnect race from exclusion in the US. Critical race scholars remind us of the permanence of racism in US society, and CRT founder Derrick Bell makes the point that race is inextricably connected with citizenship, which signifies inclusion predominantly for whites. In an article revisiting *Brown vs. Board of Education*, Bell explains that the Constitution was written with the idea in mind that "property in slaves should not be exposed to danger under a government instituted for the protection of property" ("Brown . . . Forty-Five Years" 175). Because slaves were considered property in the context of the Constitution, then citizenship was by default for white property owners. In "Whiteness as Property," Cheryl Harris identifies whiteness as the defining characteristic of citizenship and the right to exclude: "The right to exclude was the central principle, too, of whiteness as identity, for mainly whiteness has been characterized, not by an inherent unifying characteristic, but by the exclusion of others deemed to be 'not white'" (1736). In rhetorical terms, whiteness serves as a Burkean terministic screen in terms of who is allowed access to property and who is denied.

In *The Border Crossed Us*, Cisneros argues that borders and citizenship perform an "us" and "them" dialectic that follows Harris's white/nonwhite binary of exclusion. Cisneros explains that "citizenship provides a sense of identity—an organizing logic for a political and cultural community—by indexing the difference between 'us' and 'them'" (5–6). However, some push back on the delineation offered by Cisneros when discussing migrants. Johanna Hartelius considers this binary reductive: "While one could say that the immigrant 'other' negatively delineates the citizenry, this would be reductive. . . . To say that the American public understands immigrants as 'not us' obfuscates the complexity of the issue" (6). The use of the us/them binary, while reductive, remains an enduring heuristic for understanding the perceived threat of the nonwhite noncitizen. The complexity of immigration as more than categories of "good" and "bad" migrants can be more difficult to discern with the United States' escalation from deporting migrants to imprisoning them.

The separation of children from their parents at the border as part of the Trump administration's "zero tolerance" policy is a clear example of behavior that frames migrants as "them," treating them in ways many white US citizens find unimaginable. This inhumane treatment of migrants can be seen in the early 1990s when Proposition 187 threatened to cut off emergency medical services and education to undocumented migrants (Ruben Garcia). In the case of Prop 187, the detrimental consequences of a law targeting migrants are clearly life-threatening because of the emergency services that would be blocked. At the same time, cutting off education from children supports the understanding about how with citizenship "the excluded Other shapes the boundaries of inclusion" (Ribero, "Citizenship" 36), with schools and hospitals serving as those internal borders.

32 • CHAPTER 1

The following sections move into some of California's historical prece-
dents that demonstrate how race factors into policy before centering on the
Bay Area's recent history. Discussing CRT and immigration policy, Michael
A. Olivas offers some cursory examples of exclusionary policy for Indigenous,
Asian, and Latinx peoples based on race:

> Cherokee removal and the Trail of Tears; Chinese laborers and the Chinese
> Exclusion Laws; and Mexicans in the Bracero Program and Operation Wet-
> back. These three racial groups share different histories of conquest, exploi-
> tation, and legal disadvantage; but even a brief summary of their treatment
> of United States law shows commonalities of racial animus, legal infirmity,
> and majority domination of legal institutions. (11)

Olivas's attention to the Trail of Tears and the forcible removal of Indigenous
tribes from their lands speaks to what caused many of the adult immigrant
students from Guatemala to come to the US. In *The Border Crossed Us,* Cisneros cogently encapsulates the gray area Mexicans occupied with regard to
citizenship during US expansion, following the Treaty of Guadalupe-Hidalgo:
"Newly colonized Mexicans negotiated their U.S. citizenship with their Anglo
fellow citizens, struggling to articulate a middle ground between Mexican and
U.S. American racial and colonial logics" (15). The unsettling "middle ground"
Cisneros uses to describe US citizenship for Mexicans living in the US following the US-Mexico War endures as the tacit promise of inclusion in the
American Dream, continually experienced by migrants new to the US. Activist migrant groups like the Dreamers called on the Obama administration to
make good on the American Dream. However, because of the continued defer-
rals of action to be taken by those in power, rhetorical scholars have noted how
the Dreamer activism "troubled the primacy of the nation-state and citizenship, . . . refused to adhere to respectability politics, . . . forwarded embodied
identity and transnational belonging, and . . . looked for liberation in community—not solely in legislative action" (Ribero, *Dreamer* 7). The Dreamers have
no doubt learned through their own histories and experiences that they cannot
simply wait for policies to do what is right without explicit provocation.

BAY AREA HISTORY OF EXCLUSION

The history of exclusion in the Bay Area speaks to the history of similar exclusionary policies in the rest of the United States. Most anthropologists desig-
nated the Indigenous people in the East and South Bay area as "Costanoan"

(L. Field "Unacknowledged" 86), while the people have been calling themselves "Ohlones" for more than a century (Muwekma Ohlone Indian Tribe), and "Muwekwa" was used into the 1930s (Leventhal et al.). Since the arrival of the Spanish to the New World, the Indigenous Ohlone "Muwekma members were involuntarily confined at three Bay Area missions" (Nijmeh). Colonial acts of segregation were further fortified by racist legislation that determined who had rights to the land. Rhetoric and immigration scholars Emily Ironside and Lisa Corrigan describe the impact of this policy entrenching exclusion: "Since the Naturalization Act of 1790, exclusion of the feared immigrant 'Other' has been deeply entrenched in American legal history through assertions of inclusion and exclusion" (159). In *The Devil in Silicon Valley: Northern California, Race, and Mexican Americans,* Stephen Pitti examines historical data to show how violence has been a tool for those in power, beginning with the Spanish missionaries inflicting violence against Native people under the guise of civilizing them. Pitti traces the history of racism back to the colonial period in California, explaining that "ideologies of racism were imported into the valley by the Spanish, and a graduating scale of political and labor practices whose most consistent motif was violence and its threat became the norm" (2). The Ohlone Indigenous population spanning from Monterey Bay to the San Francisco Bay, referred to as "Costanoan" by Spanish colonists, suffered large losses of life because of the missions. Historian John Bean attributes the high number of deaths—something like 60,000—to disease, but he also notes that unsanitary living conditions and harsh lifestyle changes, such as diet, contributed to mortality rates often thought of as coming only from unfamiliar diseases like measles and smallpox. Still, one of the factors that remained as an enduring point of contention beyond religious ideology was the question of property and who owned the land the missions occupied.

The struggle for land and the colonial myths of Manifest Destiny and white supremacy continued throughout California's history of excluding and marginalizing nonwhites. The US-Mexican War from 1846 to 1848 was fought over what is now the Southwest: California, Arizona, New Mexico, Texas, Nevada, Utah, and Wyoming. After the US-Mexican War and the Treaty of Guadalupe-Hidalgo in 1848, the gold rush was in full swing in California, a former Mexican territory where people of Mexican heritage, or Californios, had been living alongside Native populations as well as Asian and white settlers from eastern states. Historian Rudolfo Acuña identifies the public discourse targeting nonwhites during this period: "General Persifor F. Smith in 1849 published a circular labeling noncitizens trespassers and advocating fines and imprisonment of trespassers" (140). Instead of a religious colonial ideology that the Spanish missionaries used to justify their violence, racist

34 • CHAPTER 1

ideology supported discrimination against nonwhites, becoming concretized through legislation that excluded noncitizens. Ironside and Corrigan point out the tacit designation of what constitutes a white citizen that Latinx citizens experienced: "Although racially coded as 'white' at the time of the original annexation of Mexican territory in 1848, new citizens were still interpolated as 'Mexican' well into the twentieth century, complicating their citizenship narrative" (166–67).

During the full swing of the California gold rush that contributed to the development of the Bay Area, the Foreign Miners' Tax was passed by the state legislature in 1850, stipulating that miners of Mexican and Asian heritage were "taxed $20 per month," even though not all of these miners were foreign-born (Acuña 140). Historian Linda Heidenreich points to the Foreign Miners' Tax of 1850 as evidence that "many Euro-Americans exhibited a strong animosity toward Latinos/as" (194). Ironside and Corrigan argue that the Foreign Miners' Tax performed a nationalist purpose of exclusion for the benefit of white laborers because "white laborers believed that nonwhite foreign laborers threatened the underlying class entitlements that the narrative of exclusionary nationalism had secured for them" (162–63). Written legislation sanctioned physical violence against Latinxs, specifically, as "from 1848 to 1879, according to recent studies, one out of every 3,540 ethnic Mexicans living in the Southwest was lynched at the hands of Euro-Americans" (Heidenreich 194). Lynching has always been performance of white citizenship, Ersula Ore argues in her *Lynching: Violence, Rhetoric, and American Identity,* and it was often supported by anti-Black laws. Ore explains that "legislative appeals to a racially exclusive citizenry coupled with a vested interest in retaining a white racial state instigated conditions that made the lynching of black citizens a revered performance of white citizenship identity" (32). During Trump's presidential campaigns, his dog-whistle xenophobia about "Mexico not sending their best" and calls to "build the wall" served to perform white citizenship to the exclusion of anyone below the border through implications of criminality that Trump promised to punish punitively in his isolationist rhetoric.

Between these historical exclusionary policies and more contemporary manipulation of policy affecting migrant workers, more flagrant antimigrant policies like Prop 187 in California have been passed, a policy that specifically denied health care to undocumented people. Johanna Hartelius explains that this draconian approach that

> in the 1990s was institutionalized in such severely criminalizing legislation as the Antiterrorism and Effective Death Penalty Act and the Illegal Immigration Reform and Immigrant Responsibility Act . . . operates in tandem

with an enforcement-through-attrition model, penalizing individual immigrants or immigrant groups so harshly as to have a discouraging effect. (8)

Hartelius explains that the Immigration Reform and Control Act was "commonly lauded for providing amnesty to hundreds of thousands of long-term undocumented residents. It also cracked down on future migrants, heightened border militarization, and added a provision to immigration law to summarily remove 'criminal' aliens" (75). Categories like "criminal aliens" support the reductive us/them binary that the "good" and "bad" migrant immigration policies reinstantiate. In the next section, the more complicated ways the Silicon Valley uses noncitizen labor are discussed to demonstrate how exclusion rhetorically operates through the tech industry's boosterism and manipulation of policy to rewrite the exploitation of noncitizen labor in a consumer-friendly narrative.

CONTEMPORARY BAY AREA EXCLUSION

The "good" migrant stories coming out of the Silicon Valley would have most people believe the Bay Area is completely disconnected from its historically discriminatory relationship with nonwhites and migrants alike. Since the 2016 presidential election, the Silicon Valley public relations narratives about foreign-born workers and start-ups have returned as a rhetorical topos, no doubt in response to the xenophobic "build a wall" rhetoric of Trump's campaign. The narratives, however, obscure the reality of Indigenous erasure and how average highly skilled foreign workers actually function within the tech industry. In the San Jose periodical the *Mercury News,* reporter Michelle Quinn reiterates statistics and values that appear in other news stories:

> More than one out of every three people in Silicon Valley is foreign born, according to the Silicon Valley Institute of Regional Studies. Of workers in computer and mathematical fields in the region, 67 percent were born outside the US. And immigrants have started more than half of the 87 so-called "unicorns," startups valued more than $1 billion, according to the National Foundation for American Policy, an immigration research group.

Quinn and others (Koh; Ovide) cite the same study from the National Foundation for American Policy with regard to the contributions of foreign-born workers. The repetition of these stats stands as a testament to the efficacy of public relations messaging that controls the narratives of the Silicon Valley tech industry. Rhetorically, the "good" model migrant populations described in this research describe "documented immigrants [who] still receive positive reactions to their immigration status in the United States because they often are perceived as giving more to society than they are taking from it" (Espinosa-Aguilar 158). Within this discussion of migrants, the racist us/them binary construction of citizenship can be seen in how the "skilled" computer worker migrant is compared to the "unskilled" laborer migrant, making the occlusion of the unskilled laborer socially acceptable.

While the tech industry persuasively brands their model migrants for their economic contributions, Silicon Valley insiders have been more critical about the treatment of migrant workforces. Comparing the use of migrant workers in the Silicon Valley to slave labor, former Facebook employee Antonio García Martínez describes the immigration H-1B visa system as "this bustling slave market, echoing with the clink of leg irons and auctioneer's cry" (70). Leading up to this slave labor comparison, García Martínez explains how the manipulation of H-1B visas allows migrant labor to be the lifeblood of Silicon Valley: "By paying them relatively slim H-1B-stipulated salaries while eating the fat consultancy fees, such companies get rich off the artificial employment monopoly created by the visa barrier . . . [;] everyone's on the take, including government, which charges thousands for filing fees" (70). García Martínez describes the role of H-1B visas as a part of the "institutionalized lies" that are part and parcel of the tech industry's neocolonial operating system.

Although García Martínez's *Chaos Monkeys* was sold as a provocative book about the Silicon Valley's dirty underbelly, his harsh criticism of H-1B visas helps explain why scholars have been similarly critical of these visas in the past. In 2003 Norman Matloff, a professor of computer science at the University of California at Davis, came to similar conclusions about Silicon Valley's economic motivations for H-1B visa usage running counter to their promoted claims about worker shortages and hiring the best. Matloff explains that the tech industry's "desire to hire the world's 'best and brightest' or to hire workers with a PhD, are also not supported by the data" (817). He concludes that "the employers' perceived 'shortage' was a shortage of cheap labor, not a shortage of workers" (863). In his advocacy of visa reform, Matloff describes H-1B visas as a form of indentured servitude that has been manipulated by the tech industry's lobbyists and public relations:

> The H-1B program has a long history of abuse by IT employers of all types and sizes. The abuse is largely, but not exclusively, due to the *de facto* indentured servitude of the H-1Bs. Meanwhile, the industry lobbyists have . . . engaged in massive public relations campaigns that claim IT labor shortages of various kinds, claims that have proven to be false. The bottom line is that

the industry wants H-1Bs as a source of cheap, compliant workers who will gladly work 14-hour days. (99)

Matloff's extensive empirical study of statistical data related to hiring practices offers evidence showing how immigrant labor exploitation is systemic within the tech industry. In 2013 an article in *Computer World* examined government data and concluded that "the largest single users of H-1B visas are offshore outsourcers, many of which are based in India, or, if U.S. based, have most employees located overseas" (Thibodeau and Machlis). In the same article, the *Computer World* reporters quote a public policy professor at the Rochester Institute of Technology, Ron Hira, confirming that "this is just affirmation that H-1B has become the outsourcing visa" (Thibodeau and Machlis). Even with this research and journalism shining a light on Silicon Valley's practices that manipulate a visa meant to help migrant workers, the repeated narratives about foreign-born workers ignore how H-1B visas are used for outsourcing and as de facto indentured servitude.

Perhaps as a corollary to the use of H-1B visas for offshore work, companies such as Apple, Evernote, and Zillow have admitted their lack of diverse hiring practices, which speaks to how exclusion in the form of racial segregation manifests in the tech industry. In a *Washington Post* article entitled "Silicon Valley Struggles to Hack Its Diversity Problem," Cecilia Kang and Todd Frankel explain that "Yahoo disclosed last week that African Americans made up just 2 percent of its workers, while Hispanics stood at 4 percent." Kang and Frankel reference the Associated Press and Reuters as sources reporting that "Yahoo, Facebook and Google have all disclosed low minority hiring numbers in recent months." For tech workers of color, exclusion can also play out in wage discrepancy. Citing a Joint Venture report, Andrew Ross points out that "African American and Latino residents earn 70% less than the region's top earners . . . [;] female professionals make 40% less than male counterparts." Discriminatory ideology becomes concretized through the material wage discrepancies that correspond with the exclusion from tech industry jobs. Income inequality along racial lines furthermore aligns with the increased visibility of white nationalist ideology in the Silicon Valley that became evident as it was normalized through rebranding as the "alt-right" (Miller).

CRIMINAL INDENTURED SERVITUDE

Some of the Central American migrants Mateo worked with experienced a different kind of indentured servitude. When Mateo helped young men from Central America who ran into problems with the law, he told me, "A lot of young men are unable to find work when they get here, so they are recruited to sell crack in the Tenderloin [area of San Francisco]." Upon release from juvenile detention, these young migrants moved in with Mateo in the Mission District of San Francisco, where he helped them find work and a supportive community. Becoming caught up in the legal system, these young men can then have difficulty finding legitimate work, leaving them desperate and with few options other than to return to selling drugs. According to the survey data I collected, 25 percent found immigration laws "too confusing," while more than 25 percent felt these laws "hurt all immigrant families" or "hurt Latinos." With many primarily concerned about finding work, navigating the confusing US immigration system can be overwhelming, which is no doubt by design. Access to citizenship functions much like a Burkean terministic screen where the language of the bureaucratic process "reduce[s] the number of available spots of legal entry" or "make[s] the process of becoming a legal immigrant, and maintaining this status, more onerous"—promising "opportunity, while making that promise as difficult as possible to fulfill by creating a variety of administrative burdens" (Moynihan et al. 22). These administrative burdens compound the intimidating process of legal immigration, which also asks that the migrants learn English. Adult students at the Sanctuary would sometimes struggle to learn English, not because they "lacked grit" or "did not want to work hard," but because they had little access to literacy education in their first languages, making the acquisition of another language more daunting.

In his criticism of the free market economy, Pope Francis calls on communities to address social inequalities that contribute to crime: "The hearts of many people are gripped by fear and desperation, even in the so-called rich countries. The joy of living frequently fades, lack of respect for others and violence are on the rise, and inequality is increasingly evident" (42). The crime these migrant youth turn to unfortunately plays into the rhetoric of criminality used in white supremacist efforts to exclude nonwhites from US citizenship. Karma Chávez argues that these young migrants are at risk from becoming caught up in the criminal justice system before they even choose selling drugs out of desperation. Chávez brings attention to racial profiling by police: "Being targeted as criminal by police also puts such people at higher risk of eventually being caught up in some aspect of the prison-industrial complex. If one speaks English with a non-US 'accent,' doesn't speak English at all, or frequents parts of town where immigrants are known to go, this compounds the risk" (73).

In survey data I collected at the Sanctuary, a third of the students agreed that the American Dream was possible, although more than a third believed it difficult to achieve, with one commenting that the American Dream does not exist. While this data captures a mixed snapshot of migrant feelings prior to the Trump administration, writing and critical race scholar Aja Martinez further unpacks how access to the American Dream is complicated by race. In "'The American Way': Resisting the Empire of Force and Color-Blind Racism," Martinez examines the writing of students who use cultural racism to account for the success of racial groups: "[A student] then blames the victims (a form of minimization) for not setting their standards high enough, and, at the same time, he employs cultural racism by way of assuming that all members of this racial group do not make the effort needed for American Dream success" (592). While the migrants surveyed were following a path toward assimilation through English literacy, their barrier to entry of citizenship was further fraught with racial discrimination and xenophobia. This barrier would become more evident with overt "make America great again" rhetoric that would unapologetically delineate for whom the American Dream was meant. The indentured servitude these young migrants experience once they are caught in the criminal justice system can be better understood by the role racial profiling plays in the policing of these populations who feel excluded from traditional labor opportunities.

CONCLUSION: LIMITING EXCLUSION

When I first visited Mateo in 2008, his missionary organization asked him to run a halfway house for immigrant youth he met in juvenile detention, where he offered Bible study. At that time the halfway house was in the Mission District of San Francisco. By 2013 Mateo had to move to the East Bay because gentrification had raised the cost of living for those Mateo worked with. While "gentrification" is often used as a buzzword, the history of the Bay Area reveals how migrants from Latin America, native-born Latinxs, Indigenous populations, African Americans, and Asian Americans have been marginalized from the colonizing Catholic Church, vigilante pioneers, and state-legislated discrimination.

The Bay Area has also been a space that has embodied the concept of sanctuary and confronted exclusion as the next generation seeking their fortune disrupts existing ecologies and communities. San Francisco artists Sergio De la Torre and Chris Treggiari have used exhibitions for their Sanctuary City Project to ask the questions "What is a Sanctuary? What would you tell an immigrant?" (Ramirez 178). As a part of their art, De la Torre and Treggiari have hung banners that also ask, "Where will people go?" (Ramirez 180). As homes become property investments and families are pushed from neighborhoods like the Mission District, it stands to reason that the number of unhoused people will increase as homes become investments that fewer and fewer can afford. Silicon Valley tech bros will bemoan the state of San Francisco because of increases in crime and homelessness, although they overlook their own culpability in displacing the communities who contributed to the epistemologies, culture, and ethos of the space.

The economy of exclusion in California is a part of colonial history and our neocolonial present, when migrants continue to be criminalized and framed as the Other in relation to white citizenship. Antonio's question about what can be done for him speaks for many of those seeking refuge in our country. As a literacy educator, I can help people learn the language used by those in power, though with little guarantee of their accessing that power. In this chapter, CRT reveals how exclusion operates through the promise of citizenship kept at a distance, complicated by visa abuses and public relations boosterism. In the next chapter, the intersection of CRT with decolonial theory, methods, and practices further brings to light what I call decolonial CRT tenets that help address issues specific to Indigenous populations like the Maya migrants at the Sanctuary. Building on CRT tenets, the decolonial focus brings attention to land displacement and its connection with decolonial knowledge.

The story of the Sanctuary is the story of migrant labor working hard, taking steps toward citizenship, recovering from displacement, only to experience heightened levels of criminalization. Perhaps Antonio—like many others from Guatemala and Central America—was leery of the violence that can occur without reason or warning. Judith Zur reminds us how, like Bishop Juan Gerardi Conedera, who was assassinated in Guatemala City, "the British-trained, Guatemalan anthropologist Myrna Mack Chang . . . was murdered outside her office. Myrna's 'crime' was to denounce the appalling living conditions of internal refugees" (3). As researchers, we follow protocols to protect vulnerable populations, although experience asks, *Who will protect the researcher when confronted with violence that follows a logic of terror?* What do we have to offer students like Antonio in the ongoing legacies of violence? And if we can protect ourselves, can we still be expected to protect our students from the cultural violence exchanged for the promise of literacy that we tacitly represent in these colonial sites?

CHAPTER 2

Decolonizing Immigration with Critical Race Theory

INTRODUCTION: TRUMP, WHITE SUPREMACY, ANTI-IMMIGRANT RHETORIC

In a 2014 *Los Angeles Times* article, the Sanctuary's pastor and other church leaders were interviewed about sanctuary efforts in response to the large number of unaccompanied minors from Central America. Highlighting the intersection of religious beliefs and immigration, the article described the Sanctuary church's contemporary reenactment of the Christmas story that included a

> candlelight procession [that] told a contemporary tale much on the minds of congregants. Participants portrayed a Honduran family escaping gang violence and extortion, in a nod to the thousands of unaccompanied Central American minors and families with young children who have recently traveled to the United States, where they await court proceedings. (Romney)

The culturally relevant reimagining of the traditional Christmas story of seeking refuge speaks to the deeper level of engagement of the coordinating churches and the Sanctuary with the migrant populations they serve. The Sanctuary's version of the Christmas story follows in the tradition of politically oriented Latinx theater like El Teatro Campesino, formed during the

41

farmworker strikes organized by César Chávez in Delano, California. Theater scholar Elizabeth Rodriguez Fielder describes the efficacy of performance as the rhetorical identification between performer and audience: "Theater acted—and still acts—as a conduit to other cultures that shared similar ideals: a performativity of connectedness" (108). The familiar Christmas story communicates a connection across cultures, potentially exposing audiences to social realities in Central America many may be unaware of, while potentially offering a glimpse of another reality that is possible.

My time at the Sanctuary came in the middle of a period of exponential increases of migrants from El Salvador, Guatemala, and Honduras (Taft-Morales). In 2018 these increases became visible because of the caravans, with estimates of between five and seven thousand migrants coming up through Mexico from Central America to seek asylum ("AP Explains"). The explanation by the Associated Press echoes the exigence behind the Christmas story acted out at the Sanctuary: "Dozens of Central American migrants have been kidnapped by gangs demanding money or shaken down by police. Some have been killed along the way" ("AP Explains"). Trump used his social media platform to criticize the caravans, using the asylum seekers as another opportunity to espouse isolationist policy that stood in contrast with the United States' previous asylum protocols. Paul Wickman Schmidt at Georgetown Law School explains how Trump between 2017 to 2019 severely cut US refugee admissions: "The refugee admissions ceiling set yearly by the president fell from 110,000 to 30,000 . . . the lowest ceiling since the creation of the US Refugee Admissions Program in 1980" (94). Trump's asylum policy follows in the neocolonial tradition of championing globalization and transnational business without taking accountability for the repercussions. While immigration remains a rhetorical commonplace with familiar arguments that accompany the topic, Trump's racist rhetoric actionized white supremacist logic that criminalized nonwhite migrants in ways that highlight citizenship's connection to whiteness and the right to exclude.

For years caravans of undocumented migrants from Central America made the trip north "to draw attention to the plight of Central American migrants" ("AP Explains"), using their group size and numbers for protection. Trump and conservative media purposefully conflated the caravan with Mara Salvatrucha, MS-13 gang members; Trump commented via social media: "Go into the middle of the caravan, take your cameras and search. Okay? Search. . . . You're going to find MS-13, you're going to find Middle Eastern, you're going to find everything" (Rizzo). Even though caravans, such as the one Trump is referring to, were meant to offer protection for many women and children traveling alone, Trump appealed to people subscribing to the xenophobia of white supremacist ideology, labeling these migrants as non-white "Others" known for violence. Ailsa Winton explains in her research "Youth, Gangs and Violence" how *maras* (gangs) are often, in fact, responsible for the violence that causes many migrants, including those in caravans, to seek refuge. As she states, "the upsurge in social (and often economic) violence is commonly blamed on the proliferation of youth gangs, or 'maras,' which have become an important concern in Guatemala, particularly in urban areas" (170). While the recognition of Central American gang violence could have served to explain the reason for the caravans, the president used the idea of MS-13 to appeal to the white supremacist ideology of his political base, who supported framing nonwhite migrants as potentially dangerous criminals. In *The Border Crossed Us,* Josue Cisneros explains that "securing the border" rhetoric serves as a xenophobic call to restrict citizenship: "Since borders define the parameters of citizenship, attempts to tighten borders, such as those of the Minutemen or of anti-immigrant legislators, serve to restrictively define citizenship and civic identity" (7). Calls to reinforce borders against nonwhite noncitizens serve as exigency for investigating the possibilities of decolonial approaches and critical race theory to understand, and potentially reenvision, what Guatemalan Maya migrants are up against when seeking refuge.

In this chapter I outline what I call decolonial critical race theory tenets to address white supremacist policy that impacts US and transnational Indigenous populations, displaced by neocolonial projects of capitalism. The synergy of decolonial theory and CRT could be understood as a grounded theory that "develop[s] new concepts, often linking many ideas not previously connected" (Martin et al. 13) for the purpose of articulating factors and tensions for migrating and seeking refuge against the backdrop of racially motivated discrimination and exclusion designed within the legal system of the US. For this book the concept of sanctuary speaks to the role of the church for those seeking assistance, and it also names the Spanish-speaking church buildings, particularly in relation to the English-speaking church that occupies the same property. With grounded theory, there is a "study of a concept (Glaser, 2010). The concept explains observed patterns. Through constant comparisons of data, researchers build more and more abstract concepts that they eventually integrate around the core concept" (Martin et al. 13). While decolonial theory and CRT are well known and not "abstract concepts," the underlining ideologies that inform their practices integrate around the concept of sanctuary at this site where Indigenous migrants continue to face threats of displacement, in part because of how property aligns with whiteness.

Though I am not the first to draw attention to mixing these methodologies, I do so with an eye to Latin America (à la Olson) to reveal further the matrices of oppression impacting Indigenous migrants while imagining different worlds of possibility. This work is based in CRT's call to challenge dominant ideologies (second tenet) and to create opportunities for generative intersections of anticolonial and antiracist critique to converge. One such example I build on is Ali Meghji's "Towards a Theoretical Synergy." I appreciate the intellectual labor of Meghji's advocacy for the synergistic potential of these frameworks in response to discrimination-based policy inside and outside the US: "Trump's campaign, therefore, was not only committed to giving back valuation to white citizens who felt marginalized in their own country (as CRT shows), but also giving valuation back to the nation on a global scale (which decolonial thought can show)" (9). The Trump administration came into office at the end of my time at the Sanctuary. However, the effective circulation of his racist rhetoric preceding and during his presidential campaign signals the wider acceptance of racial discrimination and foreshadows the rhetoric materializing into policies that separated families and put children into caged detention centers. In the following sections, I outline the decolonial CRT tenets that respond to these intersecting issues of race/ethnicity, immigration, language, and land that affect the predominantly Indigenous Guatemalan student population at the Sanctuary.

MIXED CRT AND DECOLONIAL METHODOLOGIES

As early as 1998, rhetoric scholars advocated for the integration of CRT into rhetoric scholarship when Marouf Hasian and Fernando Delgado explained that "combining the theoretical insights of rhetoricians and critical race theorists can help us move beyond simple and reductive ways of essentializing race and race relations" (246). Jumping nearly twenty-five years ahead, I further articulate how the tenets of CRT serve writing studies and decolonial projects addressing transnational migration. Before postulating their decolonial possibilities, I begin with the list of critical race theory tenets:

1. Permanence of race and racism
2. Challenge to dominant ideologies
3. Interest convergence
4. Race as social construct
5. Intersectionality and antiessentialism
6. Interdisciplinarity
7. Centrality of experiential knowledge and/or unique voices of color
8. Commitment to social justice (Kynard 4; A. Martinez, *Counterstory* 9; Solórzano and Delgado Bernal 314; Taylor 74).

All of the tenets are important for their application to the transnational issue of immigration and the material realities of Indigenous peoples outside as well as inside the US.

The racist policies impacting migrants attempting to enter the US as well as the many interconnected transnational countries and business interests impacted by xenophobic executive decision-making speak to a need for imagining pluriversal possibilities around a concept like sanctuary and beyond the limitations of the reality we are presented. That one of the goals of decolonial scholars is to work to imagine an alternative world and that these worlds are possible stem from Arturo Escobar's thinking on the pluriversal. He states that "another world is possible because another real and another possible are possible. That other world is a world where many worlds fit, or the pluriverse" (ix). Even though Trump's racist rhetoric shows the need for critical race theory and decolonial methodologies across different sites of inquiry within this book, Escobar's arguments for the pluriversal suggest realities grounded in rhetoric outside of a legal system and foreign policy that were not designed for Black, Indigenous, and people of color. Escobar asks that we think beyond a single reality, and this ability to do so "will help us to derealize the realist that each of us carries within ourselves, and to think-live with a more complex and effective awareness of the inexhaustible *tejido* (weave) of interdependence that sustains life and allows it to flourish, which is to say, the pluriverse" (7). The integration of CRT and decolonial theory performs an epistemological dualism that functions because it is possible for CRT realities and decolonial realities to exist both on their own as well as relationally together to engage the local and transnational.

Sociologist Ali Meghji posits mixing the methodologies of CRT and decolonial thought as a synergy where "the two can be used in tandem to provide lucid analysis of social realities" (6). I build on the work of my fellow rhetoric and writing studies scholars like Andrea Riley Mukavetz, who acknowledges the connection between decolonial theory and CRT when she describes teaching decolonial theory and methodology as showing students the "constellated understanding of decolonial theory and . . . its connections with postcolonial theory, indigenous studies, critical race theory, local knowledges and grassroots movements, and queer studies" (126). Below I further add to these discussions by articulating what I call decolonial tenets of CRT as a grounded theory centered around the concept of sanctuary. In doing so I acknowledge that these tenets come directly from the established tenets of CRT included above. The purpose of my rearticulation is to underscore where the relations, synergy, and pluriversality of the approaches intersect and provide particular focus on the transnational element immigration introduces into the US-centered attention of CRT. The decolonial tenets of CRT are as follows:

1. CRT and decolonial methods both affirm the persistence of racism as discursive and material phenomena in both the US and elsewhere impacted by the legacy of colonialism and neocolonialism.
2. CRT and decolonial methods challenge dominant ideologies reflecting imperialist and white supremacist conditions from which to delink and imagine pluriversal realities.
3. Interest convergence reaffirms the focus on Black and Indigenous roles in issues related to BIPOC communities.
4. Race is a social construct that colonialism spread throughout Indigenous communities, often to divide Native populations.
5. Intersectionality and antiessentialism resist interdependent marginalization, with particular emphasis on the topic of land and erasure through settler colonialism.
6. The interdisciplinary nature of CRT work and the pluriversal/relationality of decolonial thought work toward the inclusion of multiple knowledges and possible worlds.
7. Experiential knowledge and storytelling by BIPOC voices are central.
8. CRT and decolonial methods commit to social justice and redressing colonial legacies of injustice.

Below I further articulate these tenets, many in relation to the social realities of the predominantly Maya students at the Sanctuary.

PERSISTENCE OF RACISM

The racist conflation of migrant caravans with MS-13 by President Trump highlights how racism continues circulating in discourses and shows the need for different knowledge and potential realities. The reification of this rhetoric into the "zero tolerance" family separation policy demonstrates the material consequences of racism on immigration and the protection of white settler property at the expense of nonwhites. This foundational tenet of CRT works with decoloniality to explain how many migrants have already been victims of racism in their home countries, which bear the burdens of colonial legacies. In Guatemala—as in other Latin American countries—racism was institutionalized as a legitimate delineation between Spanish-speaking Ladinos and Indigenous Maya. Research in Guatemala suggests that many of the Indigenous Maya have internalized this racism: "Their servility in the face of overt racism, make[s] it seem as though Mayas have accepted their subservient role in Guatemalan society" (Green 68). Others have characterized the "civil war" / *la violencia* as a systematic effort by the US-backed Ladino government to commit genocide because it was an organized effort to eradicate the Indigenous Maya (Sanford; Torres). In their book on Guatemalan migrants in the Midwest, Ann Sittig and Martha Florinda González explain that "the hatred with which some Ladinos treat the Mayans cannot be denied, and the racism underlying the genocidal war is still omnipresent in Guatemala" (42). Critical race theory's emphasis on racism as permanent and persistent helps articulate racism's role in contexts where communities attempt to untangle or delink (à la Mignolo "Delinking") ways of thinking, offering pluriversal worlds apart from those where racist paradigms have been instituted through colonialism and entrenched through the neocolonial thirst for the accumulation of capital.

CHALLENGE TO DOMINANT IDEOLOGIES

My limited ability to effect change for the adult students at the Sanctuary, as demonstrated by the student Antonio in chapter 1, underscores the need for subverting, resisting, and challenging dominant ideologies that limit our imaginations in terms of what is possible. As an ideological apparatus, the Sanctuary creates a space for marginalized migrants to acquire the dominant language of English and imagine alternative worlds. However, this relationship between church and language further evidences how dominant narratives about the "good" migrant are supported by racial assimilation that is intrinsically intertwined with the extent to which a migrant can language in the dominant discourse. The second tenet of CRT, challenging dominant ideologies, accounts for legacies of colonialism and their enduring effects: "A second tenet of CRT that raises awareness of the alternative perspectives and cultural interpretations that linguistic minorities bring to their learning is the importance placed on understanding the historic effects of European colonialism (Bell 1980; Crenshaw 1988; Taylor et al. 2009)" (Liggett 116). For students at the Sanctuary, colonialism has historically imposed the Spanish language on them, and neocolonial transnational business caused many of them to migrate, thereby imposing yet another dominant language. CRT scholars Richard Delgado and Jean Stefancic include colonial plundering of natural resources as an important consideration and relevant to the purview of critical race studies: "U.S. and European colonialism robbed the former colonies of their natural wealth, suppressed the development of local leaders, and conspired with rightwing dictators to keep the people poor, fearful, and disorganized" (125). The dominant ideology of neocolonial free market

48 · CHAPTER 2

capitalism has materialized not only in the form of "legitimate" transnational corporations like coffee and palm tree oil exporters but also more viciously in the narco-traffickers who threaten, murder, and displace Indigenous populations in countries like Guatemala where the governments have been weakened by US intervention. The land displacement Guatemalan Indigenous experience is central to decolonial approaches centering Indigeneity, and imagining a pluriverse is what Arturo Escobar articulates as a response to violence in Latin America: "In Latin America, the dominant strategies of doing away with, or at least neutralizing, difference (despite their violence) have not done away with the multiplicity of ways of worlding" (xiii). Kamala Harris chiding Guatemalans, "Do not come" to the US reveals a poverty of imagination in the ability to conceive of a world other than what will continue being re-created in the likeness of a free market that may work in theory but excludes in reality.

INTEREST CONVERGENCE

The location of the East Bay is important to consider as a geographic place and a space traditionally marginalized populations have called home. As Mateo the missionary noted, he had to move from the Mission District of San Francisco to the East Bay when the fixed-gear bike-riding Four Horsemen of the gentrification apocalypse pedaled into town. They made San Francisco no longer affordable to him or the community he served. The East Bay has traditionally had one of the largest Black populations in Northern California, and Latinxs account for a similar percentage of the overall population. So the location of the Sanctuary and the politics of the space speak to the need for the interest convergence of nonwhites in response to issues such as gentrification, environmental racism, linguistic racism, and many others. Interest convergence in decolonial projects helps underscore parallel oppressions Black and Indigenous communities continue to experience, while helping to re-center issues such as reparations for Black descendants of slavery and land rematriation for Indigenous populations.

In their article "Decolonizing Decoloniality: Considering the Mis(use) of Decolonial Frameworks in TPC Scholarship," Cana Uluak Itchuaqiyaq and Breeanne Matheson bring attention to the necessary synergy CRT and decolonial practice could serve in addressing how the history of slavery complicates decolonial attention to land displacement. As Itchuaqiyaq and Matheson explain,

> We recognize that chattel slavery has complicated issues of "homeland" and a sense of place for Black communities in the United States whose ancestors

were stolen from their homelands and brought to the US unwillingly. More work is needed to explore how sovereignty in the Black community and Indigenous community intersect and complement one another, especially in how these communities use narrative to evoke a sense of place, belonging, and identity. (27)

Sovereignty is important not only in Black and US Indigenous communities but also in transnational Indigenous communities who migrate because of a lack of sovereignty. Kyle Mays's *Afro-Indigenous History of the United States* also raises many important points related to interest convergence between Black and Indigenous peoples. As Mays argues, "The core foundations of US democracy, and white people's strong belief in its possibilities were, from the beginning, based on the subjugation of Black and Indigenous peoples. Until we as a nation . . . come to terms with this, we aren't ever really going to see any real changes" (19). This argument about the oppression of Black and Indigenous peoples echoes the tenet of interest convergence. Until the oppression of Black and Indigenous peoples ends and projects of rematriation and reparations become systemic, society will continue perpetuating historical inequalities and oppression. In a religious sense, the nation will never be able to atone for the twin sins of slavery and the genocide of Indigenous peoples. The "real change," as Mays mentions, suggests that those pluriversal realities where the entrenched systems of oppression could be rejected by communities working together address what we have been led to believe is "just the way it is." This is the kind of stock story/dominant narrative that dismisses the possibility of other worlds.

RACE AS SOCIAL CONSTRUCT

The social construction of race served projects of colonialism as a means of establishing a European or white supremacist ideology while constructing racial or ethnic differences among the colonized population. The impact of the social construction of race can be clearly seen in the lives of the Indigenous Maya in Guatemala who, as a part of assimilation, have been taught to self-identify as being of European heritage to gain power over other Indigenous Maya. It has been shown that the Ladino identity, a Guatemalan with mixed Indigenous and European heritage, is a construct through the tacit recategorization of these individuals as Ladino when Maya males joined the army. They "welcomed the role as a means of reclassifying themselves as *ladino*, appropriating the *ladino*'s power . . . [;] this self-identification encourages *jefes* to abuse and exploit fellow villagers as they themselves have been exploited by *ladinos*" (Zur 108). As

50 · CHAPTER 2

a state apparatus, the army constructs the social reality for the enlisted and imbues those within it with the power to oppress through racial discrimination. Assimilation to the dominant group—with Europeanness as the construct of desired racial difference—reveals the very false nature of the social construct.

In chapter 4 I discuss the Sanctuary's struggle over the church's lease with an English-speaking congregation who shares the lease with the Spanish-speaking congregation. The power of the English language and its alignment with whiteness allow the predominantly white, English-speaking congregation to question the legitimacy of the Sanctuary's right to their buildings. Kyle Mays offers a useful explanation for the purpose of socially constructing race in the US as coming down to the ability to own property. Mays explains that "'White' meant property owner and human, 'African and Indigenous' meant the opposite" (19). The explanation Mays offers for citizenship as an extension of race operating as a social construction follows earlier arguments by CRT scholars Derrick Bell and Cheryl Harris that highlight shared, intersectional struggles related to land as property that Indigenous peoples experience inside and outside the US.

INTERSECTIONALITY OF LAND AND PROPERTY

Intersectionalities identify matrices of issues that overlap and intersect with different communities. For transnational Indigenous migrants, the issues of language and land come into focus because they have been areas of control for systems of oppression that continue bringing to light the necessity for sovereignty and reparations. Reparations for Black communities relate to the discussion of property because African Americans were brought to this country and regarded by the laws of this country as property. The simultaneous sins of Indigenous genocide and slavery consumed Native American land while building the nation's wealth on the backs of enslaved Blacks. Notable CRT scholar Derrick Bell makes foundational articulations of how the law was written for the protection of white property, and Cheryl Harris extends Bell's work while identifying the intersecting issue of land Native Americans have experienced and continue to experience. Harris points out how race was constructed as an explanation for the seizure of land through settler colonialism: "The settlement and seizure of Native American land supported white privilege through a system of property rights in land in which the 'race' of the Native Americans rendered their first possession rights invisible and justified conquest" (1727).

My time as a volunteer educator at the Sanctuary brought the issue of property to bear through both the displacement of the migrant students and the struggle over the church's lease. It unfortunately makes sense that the battleground over CRT takes place in public education policy, even though CRT stems from the field of law, because the repercussions of racist policies are experienced by educators in underfunded and over-policed schools. Education and CRT scholars Gloria Ladson-Billings and William Tate describe the important work of Derrick Bell and his identification of the protection of property having its roots in the racist project of slavery: "Bell examined the events leading up to the Constitution's development and concluded that there exists a tension between property rights and human rights. This tension was greatly exacerbated by the presence of African peoples as slaves in America. The purpose of the government was to protect the main object of society—property" (53). Kyle Mays traces the intersecting relationship between African and Indigenous oppression to property when he writes, "The foundations of whiteness today are rooted in the twin oppressions of Africans and US Indigenous peoples. How we view race and, in the formative years of the United States, who can own and be property was rooted in these oppressions" (18). Displacement affects and has affected Indigenous populations across the Americas, and the Maya student population at the Sanctuary is no different. Property is central to the neocolonial project of gentrification that plasters a real estate agent's preening face on the signs of Western progress rewritten as "renovation," including open floor plans, horizontal fences, and gutted interiors that show no signs of what came before.

CRT reveals how the enduring legacy of racism impacts both citizenship and property rights, and decolonial theory reveals how the enduring legacy of colonialism continues to impact transnational and US issues of land and citizenship, while asking us to imagine other realities. In Guatemala, the interconnection between transnational corporations and land displacement can be traced back to US involvement in 1952, when the US government backed United Fruit Corporation's dispute with Guatemalan president Arbenz, who attempted to repatriate some of the 90 percent of land used for agricultural export. The dominant ideology in the US feared the spread of communism, so when the Guatemalan government "began the expropriation of 240,000 acres of the United Fruit Company's holdings on the Pacific Coast and 173,000 acres on the Atlantic Coast . . . the company was able to convert what was an essentially a business dispute with Guatemalan officials into an ideological conflict between the United States and countries of the Soviet bloc" (Ujpán 6). The US intervened in Guatemala's politics because of businesses interested in the extraction of the country's natural resources, with no concern for how this land grab through military support would continue destabilizing the country's infrastructure and the ability for its people to self-sustain for generations.

When discussing Guatemalan Indigenous people displaced from their lands and the Indigenous Guatemalans at the Sanctuary in the US, I do not want to erase the differences within the Indigenous communities across Guatemala. However, the history of the Guatemalan government reveals these attacks against Indigenous peoples were widespread. Andrea Riley Mukavetz helps explain the advocacy across communities when describing the interconnectedness of Indigenous space and how colonial legacies continue to impact diverse Native populations across time and space. Mukavetz argues that "indigenous space is always connected to ongoing colonial impact," and she wants to teach students "to feel that interconnectedness. This, in turn, helped them understand how decolonial practice is always localized and affective" (128). While some Indigenous Maya might not be impacted by transnational businesses displacing them because their families have moved to cities, the gang violence and their connection with narco-trafficking means Indigenous people in rural areas and cities are similarly impacted and confined by business interests that forcibly remove populations from their ancestral lands.

INTERDISCIPLINARITY

The interdisciplinary nature of CRT work and the pluriversality/relationality of decolonial thought together work toward the inclusion of multiple coexisting knowledges serving to center Indigenous traditions as sites of knowledge production. Arturo Escobar describes the acknowledgment of these multiple, paralleling sites of knowledge as tied to the "struggle over a new reality, what might be called the pluriverse, and over the designs for the pluriverse" (xii). Concerns over local issues can bring to light struggles over where the focus should be and what tradition might best inform solving a given issue. Escobar points to Afro-pessimism as an epistemology and ethical project for refusing to refuse blackness (xxvii) and that could push back against interdisciplinarity where Indigenous concerns are addressed without the concerns of Black communities. However, I argue that pluriversal worlds that refuse Blackness or synergies of CRT and decolonial thought, which always consider the intersecting oppressions of Black communities with other communities, would be fatally flawed in their imagining. We might begin to conceptualize pluriversal worlds where BIPOC centers Black and Indigenous communities, in more than acronym form, as in the realities of work like that of Kyle Mays, whose *An Afro-Indigenous History of the United States* actively engages with these parallel and overlapping histories.

In rhetoric and composition studies, scholars addressing decoloniality have advocated for pluriversality, asking us to "learn to unlearn, to 'forget what we have been taught, to break free from the thinking programs imposed on us by education, culture, and social environment, always marked by the

Western imperial reason'" (Tlostanova and Mignolo, qtd. in Cushman et al. 7–8). Similar to the Afro-pessimistic ethical imperative to center Blackness, scholars cautiously advocate for storytelling as a research method as long as it avoids "replications of knowledge hierarchy" (Cushman et al. 13). The replicated hierarchies speak to the ways Black history, knowledge, and accomplishments have been erased in the maintenance of white supremacy and Western knowledge traditions shackled to European thought. In their discussion of making relationships among rhetorical traditions, the Cultural Rhetorics Theory Lab, which came out of the Cultural Rhetorics Conference at Michigan State University, articulates how it is possible to draw on multiple traditions, such as CRT and decolonial theory: "We believe it's important to keep all traditions/stories/histories in play as equally legitimate origins and progenitors of many simultaneous rhetorical traditions. Further, we believe there is rhetorical power in building relationships between multiple traditions, multiple histories, multiple practices" (Powell et al. 7). Because CRT includes interdisciplinarity as a foundational tenet, both frameworks draw on various knowledge traditions, while centering Black pluriversality and acknowledging rhetorical sovereignty à la Scott Lyons and Lisa King.

STORYTELLING AND EXPERIENTIAL KNOWLEDGE

For CRT scholars, the stories of BIPOC individuals are central to identifying and resisting systemic racism that delegitimizes the experiences of communities of color. CRT's seventh tenet of centering experiential knowledge speaks to trusting the counterstories, composite stories, and testimonios of BIPOC. The discrimination these individuals and communities experience can often be traced to policy and other underlying social factors that undergird racism. Indigenous decolonial scholars make a similarly important argument for story and storytelling as a form of knowledge-making. Cherokee rhetoric scholar Emily Legg explains how storytelling serves to help "understand the complex rhetorical ecologies that situate participants, materials, environments, technologies, and cultural practices together" (27). Stories and narratives help illuminate the complex ecologies at the Sanctuary while also situating both the Indigenous Guatemalan students and how they came to the Sanctuary and my participation as someone taking part within this ecology.

Because immigration policy and political rhetoric dehumanize migrants like the adult students at the Sanctuary, it is necessary for stories to enter our research, when they can, in order to reframe how we see our relationship to these communities. Indigenous rhetorical scholars Lisa King, Rose Gubele, and Joyce Rain Anderson extend Cherokee author Thomas King's notion that "the stories we tell about ourselves and about our world frame our perceptions, our relationships, our actions, and our ethics" (3). Further unpacking these ideas in *Survivance, Sovereignty, and Story: Teaching American Indian Rhetorics,* they explain that "all literature, all the theorizing, all writing are part of the stories . . . the connected narrative that tells us who we are in relationship to one another" (King et al. 9). The elements of story and detail in this book do not strictly adhere to traditional ethnography, though this research underwent the university IRB process, because in many cases the elements of "story" and moments of rhetorical silence provoke important questions or demonstrate phenomena otherwise ignored. As Legg mentions, these stories come from my participation within this ecology, and my goal is that they will help reframe perspectives and understandings about people who risk their lives to seek refuge in the US and about our relationships with them.

COMMITMENT TO SOCIAL JUSTICE

During the years I volunteered at the Sanctuary, I was advised to include this teaching in the "service" category of the work I do when I submitted annual reviews at my Jesuit university. Even though social justice is explicitly stated in the mission of the university, the feedback I received was that this "community service" could not be factored into my teaching and that it was not valued in the same way as my university valued service for the department and college. I note this because a commitment to social justice as a CRT tenet, like many of these tenets, is not a given or static, but must be practiced and reconstituted through justice-seeking projects, or it can become yet another empty promise. CRT and decolonial methods seek to address the impacts of socially unjust policy and redress the impacts of colonial legacies. The migration of students from Guatemala to the Sanctuary underscores work by CRT scholars on immigration who have identified the enduring connection between citizenship and property: "Various forms of citizenship status stem from the delineation of rights, privileges, and penalties relative to property, taxes, welfare, and the freedom of movement across nation states" (M. Romero 27). What transnational migrants experience as noncitizens in the US is ultimately entangled with the unjust legal system that punishes migrants seeking refuge from injustice. Decolonial practices and knowledges can illuminate the historical projects of genocide and enduring subjugation as castoffs from free market enterprises. To call back to intersectionality, society cannot be free of social injustices when the oppression of Black and Indigenous communities continues to go unexamined as a reality of the worlds we imagine.

Having discussed the ways CRT and decolonial methodologies provide complementary approaches to reconciling how racism and colonialism continue to impact immigration in the US, I explain how these frameworks can inform methods of collecting information, analyzing data, and representing lived experiences through ethnographic description.

DECOLONIZING TRADITIONAL RESEARCH METHODS

My relationship with Mateo led me to gain trust first as a teacher at the Sanctuary, thereby allowing me to further earn trust to conduct research. In addition, my relationship with Mateo and this student population reminded me to be reflective in my practices in terms of issues such as ethical representation. In the foundational text *Decolonizing Methodologies: Research and Indigenous Peoples,* Linda Tuhiwai Smith explains that traditional research methods like interviews should be understood as a process that relies on interconnected networks where consent and trust are earned. Smith writes, "In Hawai'i kanaka Maoli, or native Hawai'ian researchers, have talked of the many aunties, uncles and elders whose views must be sought prior to conducting any interviews in a community. In Australia Aborigine researchers speak also of the many levels of entry which must be negotiated when researchers seek information" (15). During my time at the Sanctuary, I spoke with Mateo about the possibility of conducting research, and because of our friendship of fifteen years and my commitment to volunteering, he felt comfortable introducing me to Pastor Pablo and other stakeholders like Isabel, who was instrumental in the English program and everyday workings at the Sanctuary. Isabel was the first person the students and volunteer teachers would go to about anything from enrollment to room assignments, prayer requests to copies of handouts, and everything in between. As a relational practice, I continue keeping in touch with Mateo, and I have asked him for feedback on my writing to avoid putting him or the community he serves at risk.

In consideration of the Indigenous migrant student population at the Sanctuary, technical communication and decolonial scholar Godwin Agboka's work in Ghana provides additional important insight about interviews. Speaking with people in a community about the efficacy of technical documents, Agboka describes drawing on a decolonial methodology because of the role research has played in colonialism: "The underlying problem is that when research participants are seen as subjects, they become only objects to be exploited, rather than equal partners in the research process . . . [;] the term 'subjects' [should] be banned from reports on humans, because it is demeaning and smacks of colonialism" (300). While Agboka argues terms like "subjects" should not be used, he makes the point that decolonial methods can still draw on traditional sources of information. Agboka agrees with other decolonial scholars who practice the theories and methods intended for centering Indigenous knowledge: "Scholars often use the term 'decolonial' to capture the process of rupturing and challenging the political economy of knowledge production that accords certain privileges and legitimacy to certain forms of knowing while invalidating indigenous knowledges or viewpoints of research participants" (302). Decolonial practices ask researchers to maintain a level of responsibility to the research participants in the process of collecting information, but also to maintain a commitment to portray the knowledge communicated by participants ethically and accurately.

Considering the use of interviews and surveys, generally thought of as traditional qualitative and quantitative tools for data collection, Godwin Agboka pays attention to decolonial methodologies as a process, and the ethical consideration of these tools makes an important case for these methods. He explains that "decolonial researchers do not necessarily propose new data sources, but adapt these sources to the research context. For this project, methods included collection and analysis of documents, direct observations, semi-structured interviews, and focus groups with participants" (310). In this research, sources like surveys and semi-structured interviews provided some macro data like the percentage of Indigenous Mam speakers, while the interviews provided nuanced information such as the concern parents have about their child growing up and losing the ability to speak their Indigenous community's language while also recognizing the importance of learning English.

Occupying the space as a teacher-researcher, I reflected on and negotiated the relatively objective curriculum of correct and incorrect answers for the lessons, while remaining open to the topics and responses the students would offer before, between, and after classes. Decolonial scholars in rhetoric offer an important warning about "objective" approaches to research when they point out that "the 'objective' lens legitimized popular notions of white supremacy by scientifically proving the inferiority of nonwhites, greatly influencing twentieth-century notions of nationalism, citizenship, and American identity" (Ironside and Corrigan 165). CRT similarly problematizes "objective" research and logic as influenced by myths of white supremacy. Aja Martinez explains that CRT methodology challenges assumptions about the neutrality of "objective" research. Martinez writes that CRT methodology functions "as a challenge to 'majoritarian' stories or 'master narratives' of white privilege. This methodology rejects notions of 'neutral' research or 'objective' research and exposes research that silences and distorts epistemologies of people of color" (*Counterstory* 3). The question of whose knowledge and who has the ability to construct knowledge is asked in both CRT and decolonialism. In his discussion of decolonial methodologies, Agboka makes a similar case for decolonial approaches and explains that "the epistemic tradition of the functionalist school was dominated by a research approach that was uncritical, unreflexive, colonizing, and culturally-insensitive" (299). While traditional methods can have their place, as Agboka describes, decolonial practices ask the researcher to be conscious of potential repercussions of the proposed "objective" methods employed.

SURVEYS

Observations and interviews create a granular understanding of a community because of the researcher's participation and closeness as an insider within a community; however, to make certain generalizations about the student population without essentializing the nationalities, ages, genders, goals, and obstacles faced by this community, survey data help to reveal trends, or, at the very least, salient characteristics about the student population. In many cases, the data collected from surveys at the Sanctuary provided important points of departure for articulation and clarification in more informal and formal interviews as well as for understanding secondary existing scholarship on the history and social realities of Guatemala and other Central American countries. A couple different data sets I collected, in coordination with the Sanctuary's staff and volunteers, allowed me to gather demographic information, as well as potential insights into perspectives on race, language, and citizenship.

When I met with the pastor at the Sanctuary, I asked him if I could ask students to fill out surveys, letting him know I would tell the students they did not have to as a part of the English classes and that it was completely their choice. During one Monday night, before classes began, I reintroduced myself to all of the classes and told them I was conducting research. I read from an IRB-approved script, letting them know they would not be punished if they chose not to take part and that it was entirely voluntary. For the few sessions that I collected surveys, I began asking students I had known longest, reexplaining that I did research as a part of my university teaching. Most of the students who chose to fill out the surveys did so, asking a couple questions at most, sometimes asking me to clarify what I meant in a given question.

In addition to the surveys I collected at the Sanctuary, I was also given access to survey data collected by Mateo for the benefit of his outreach.

Because Mateo's work is that of a missionary, the surveys included questions regarding religious affiliation, church membership, and prayer preferences. I felt humbled by the access to surveys that included prayer requests for family safety, learning English, and finding work. Researching a large topic like immigration can feel overwhelming due to the way it intersects with so many global issues, but I found so much humanity in the basic desires for safety, the ability to provide for family, and the ability to communicate expressed in the survey that Mateo shared with me.

Other than the prayer requests that Mateo's surveys included, there were also questions about the students' levels of literacy. From these surveys, Mateo raised the concern for the teachers that some of the students had never attended any formal education. Still, the majority responded that they could write in their first language, although there was some ambiguity about whether that meant Spanish or the Indigenous language of Mam, which more than a third of respondents spoke as their first language. In Guatemala 530,000 people speak the Mayan language of Mam (Lewis et al.). There is a certain amount of irony in anti-immigration and pro-assimilation arguments by English-speaking monolinguals for migrants to *learn the language* when a significant percentage of migrants already speak one colonial language that has been imposed on them.

After collecting fifty-four surveys over the course of multiple solicitations, I coded the answers into a spreadsheet with data that would provide statistical information about the demographics, perspectives, and motivations of the student population. On first impression of reading the surveys I collected, I sensed a certain degree of fear or uncertainty in the survey responses. Because they are a vulnerable population, I understood their concern and explained prior to passing out the surveys that I would be the only one looking at the information in their responses. Still, there were some students who either left some questions unanswered or answered "prefer not to answer" for a majority of the relatively short twelve-question survey. The preference not to answer speaks loudly as an answer for a group of students who are humble and reserved in their interactions and role as students. While more traditional ethnographic researchers might enter into their "research site" with the intention of finding out revealing data about their "subjects," I did not follow up. I wanted to respect their desire not to address the violence in their home countries, especially with what I believed was my little ability to help with any dangerous situations back home that could be ongoing. For aspects relating to gangs and violence, I only reference what students shared with me unprompted or what was shared with another source with the intention of publishing this information (see Romney's *Los Angeles Times* story).

CONCLUSION

On one of the nights that I was collecting surveys at the Sanctuary, I spoke with one of my favorite students, Gerald. Many times, Gerald's eyes were bloodshot, no doubt a result of the early hours that he worked construction. He would tell me about where he was working that week, or I would ask about his younger brother who sometimes came to classes. When I asked him to fill out a survey, I told him, "My research comes from my interest in learning more about your, and everyone at the Sanctuary's, decision to come to the United States."

Despite his weary expression, Gerald was focused on learning English, moving from the beginner class to the advanced class at a pace unmatched by any other student. He had a wife and kids back in Guatemala, but he said his kids were teenagers, already with their own lives. Gerald's tireless effort in class demonstrated the selflessness of someone working hard to improve the lives of his family back home.

When he asked me about my research, I explained to him that I was interested in immigration because I had moved from Arizona, where strict laws about immigration enforcement had passed while I was there. During 2010 Arizona passed Senate Bill 1070, which allowed local law enforcement to act as federal law enforcement, giving them the ability to question anyone about their legal status based on their suspicion. The impact of these laws stayed with me as someone who lived and studied in Arizona and then returned to my home state of California because these bills inspired copycat legislation in states like Alabama, Georgia, Indiana, South Carolina, and Utah, as noted by the American Civil Liberties Union.

Racial-profiling laws are some of the overt racist phenomena that have prompted researchers in the field of sociology to take up critical race theory as a research method to help account for the racial implications of immigration policy and enforcement. In her description of Mexican migrants impacted disproportionately by enforcement, sociologist and critical race scholar Mary Romero describes someone like Gerald and many others at the Sanctuary: "Physical appearance as Latino, association with a work crew, inability to speak English or preference to speak Spanish, and proximity to the border are used as reasonable suspicion to justify investigatory stops" (29). While Romero focuses on migrants from Mexico and even the profiling of US citizens with Mexican heritage, the characteristics of "physical appearance as Latino" and "association with a work crew" bear too many similarities. The capacity to separate families and turn away asylum seekers speaks to the level of dehumanization enacted by a policy that relies on the construction of nonwhite migrants as criminals when they seek refuge and opportunities for work.

Gerald nodded his head, acknowledging that he had heard of Arizona's laws. It was 2014 and Trump had yet to begin his campaign for president on a platform that included a "build a wall" chant and other jingoistic rhetoric. When I asked Gerald if he thought California could ever have laws like Arizona, he said, "No. California is much different than Arizona."

Following the 2016 presidential election and president-elect Trump's promise to deport "at least two million," campuses and cities across the country declared themselves sanctuaries, vowing to protect undocumented students and not aid federal immigration enforcement. The certainty with which Gerald spoke has wavered for many undocumented people who once wanted to work for their version of a better life in the US.

During my time at the Sanctuary that coincided with Trump's presidential campaign, the necessity for critical race theory as a framework for understanding the white nationalist ideology at play in the rhetorical appeals to "make America great again" seemed to increase exponentially. At the same time, the closed borders isolationism in this slogan as well as "build the wall" chants underscore the need for decolonial approaches. These approaches would help us understand the impact of the United States' continuing colonial legacy that should be held accountable in countries where the US intervened in the name of democracy while protecting economic interests. Ali Meghji makes this point when he explains that "from a decolonial perspective, what we see in such arguments are attempts by Trump to reinscribe the coloniality of power, and the coloniality of knowledge" (10). Despite there being no official language in the US, colonial power argues that knowledge can only be created and communicated in English.

Critical race theory and decolonial theory provide a grounded theoretical framework for conceptualizing the interrelations among what could be seen as disparate subjects, texts, and ideas. These theories show how racism and colonial beliefs have been normalized through exclusionary policies that have served to expatriate Native populations while protecting the property of white citizens. With Joseph Biden becoming president in 2020, the US made little progress in offering aid to those seeking asylum from Central America. During her trip to Guatemala, Vice President Harris was quoted by the BBC and other news organizations as having told potential migrants: "Do not come. Do not come. The United States will continue to enforce our laws and secure our borders" ("Kamala Harris"). While Harris's proclamation avoided accusing all migrants of being gang members or criminals, her "secure our borders" rhetoric articulates what legal scholars have called "the prevention through deterrence paradigm" (Shahshahani and Gosrani 1258). In her book, *The Truths We*

Hold: An American Journey, Harris acknowledges the need for asylum seekers because of the destabilization in Central America, but critics point out how she fails to account for "the role of the US in supporting repressive regimes in El Salvador and the military government in Guatemala before and during the civil wars. Moreover, she has nothing to say about how the US-funded Contras established bases in Honduras to attack the Sandinista government in Nicaragua during the 1980s" (Bose e30). Her narrative follows a colonial tradition of benefitting from a country's natural resources while doing little to redress the aftermath of governmental intervention.

Additionally, Biden's presidential term has been characterized in many ways as continuing the dehumanizing legacy of the previous administration. However, legal scholars have noted increases in detainment, even compared with Trump's administration:

> The Biden administration has remained committed to an immigration system that inflicts harm on immigrant communities . . . [and] federal officials have in fact detained immigrants at a *greater rate* than the previous administration did, often in ICE prisons with track records for abusing and dehumanizing immigrants. (Shahshahani and Gosrani 1248; emphasis added)

Especially relevant to the Guatemalan Maya population at the Sanctuary, "the Biden administration has committed more resources to border militarism to undermine the rights of asylum seekers and indigenous migrants" (1249). The "Do not come" message of Kamala Harris is anything but empty rhetoric and should be viewed as a threat at the tip of an iceberg of heightened militarization at the border that migrants face when they venture past the surface of Harris's statement.

In the next chapter, the topic of violence provides a multilayered response to questions about the motivations of Central Americans to migrate to the US. I address the film *Sin Nombre* and other texts bringing to bear the realities of violence Central Americans experience at home and on their journey to the US. As scholars, exhuming and engaging with these legacies of violence, which the US is implicated in, can be some of the ways with which we seek to counter the erasure and silencing of these uncomfortable histories. Chapter 3 further underscores hauntings related to gender-based violence that go ignored, written off as a cost of transnational business that migrant women pay at higher rates, many times with their lives.

CHAPTER 3

Violence and the Legacy of Colonial Genocide

INTRODUCTION

The spaces for intermediate classes at the Sanctuary church are made up of a small conference room off of the pastor's office and another room on the first floor toward the entrance sometimes used for day care. Up the narrow wooden stairway, there's another meeting room with a large oval-shaped desk in the middle, and another small classroom with children's desks. The small classroom with children's desks was where the advanced class sat in a small circle with the edges of the desks so close they nearly touched. In the church basement, the introductory class took up the majority of the space, but sometimes shared it with a men's group that met on the other side of moveable walls on wheels that sectioned off the class area from the men's group. Toward the back of the basement space was the kitchen where staff and women from the church prepared coffee and cut up pieces of pan dulce during breaks in the middle of the 6 to 8 p.m. classes. In the basement, there were multiple rows of bench tables that folded up and rolled on wheels. A whiteboard and children's schoolwork as well as some university pennants lined the walls. In the most difficult of teaching circumstances, the church's band sometimes practiced above the classroom in the church's Sanctuary space, with singing, guitars, and drums providing a thumping layer of noise to speak above when talking to multiple bench tables full of students.

VIOLENCE AND THE LEGACY OF COLONIAL GENOCIDE · 63

Before and after classes, students are often on their cell phones in the same manner as students at my home institution. About a year into teaching at the Sanctuary, I walked into my intermediate classroom on the first floor, after the coffee and pan dulce break from 7 to 7:15 p.m. One of the students, Edward, was showing something to Maria, a woman who works at the church. Edward was one of the older students, in his mid- to late forties. He often had specific questions about words or phrases, asking if there are equivalent idioms to what we discussed in class. He mentioned having teenage children who speak English well.

As I got closer, he held up his phone for me to see as he had for Maria. On the screen the familiar blue outline of a social media site bordered the picture of what appeared to be images of dead bodies with cuts, wounds, and blood streaked, puddled, or stained. Edward gave me something of an apologetic smile and said the pictures came from his country, El Salvador. "The government," he said, "lost control."

I asked, "Is it gangs or drugs?"

"Both," he said. As noted in a Congressional Research Service report, an analyst for Latin American Foreign Affairs, Clare Ribando, explained that "Honduras, Guatemala, and El Salvador are at the epicenter of the gang crisis, with some of the highest murder rates in the world" (1). Edward was one of the few El Salvadorians at the Sanctuary, but his reasons for coming to the US were the same as those of many of the other students from Guatemala.

Edward came to class regularly and said he used English at work. "Kids," he said, "took pictures of the bodies and shared them online." He explained that the pictures appeared frequently on the social media timelines of friends back home the way many share news stories about politics, sports, and popular culture. As in Mexico and other Central American countries, newspapers in El Salvador have similar graphic photos of victims of the drug trade on their covers. At the same time as my conversation with Edward, the Associated Press reported that "the month of June saw 677 murders in El Salvador, more than in any other single month since the end of the country's civil war" ("El Salvador's"). Reporter Óscar Martínez interviews contract killers, displaced Indigenous people forced to work for narcos, and others who detail the institutional corruption that can do little to stop the violence in Guatemala, El Salvador, and Honduras in *A History of Violence*. Specifically, Martínez explains, "In El Salvador, the ratio is more than eighty [murders for every 100,000 inhabitants]. This month, the epidemic has been particularly bad, raging in a country of only 13,000 square miles, home to 6.2 million people, and yet averaging twenty-three murders a day. By comparison, during the sixteen-year Civil War, which ended in 1992, the average murder rate was sixteen" (xix). Even though the term "civil war" was used to reframe the geno-cide by the US-aligned Guatemalan government, at least during the "civil war" some attention was given to Central American countries to help explain the influx by those migrating. Even when Trump drew attention to the migrant caravans, he never provided context about the violence in the countries of origin, nor did he acknowledge the United States' culpability in the demand for drugs or inexpensive import costs on products such as coffee and palm oil.

Since Edward was from El Salvador, while the majority of the students at the Sanctuary came from Guatemala, I do not want to conflate the experiences in Central American countries; however, both countries share historical fac-tors that impact migration such as US intervention, civil war, drug trafficking, and widespread poverty. Unfortunately, the violence in El Salvador is some-thing Guatemalans experience as well. In another Congressional Research Ser-vice report, Maureen Taft-Morales notes that Guatemala "is considered one of the most insecure countries in the world, with a rate of 34 homicides per 100,000 people, and 76% of the population expressing little or no trust in the police [Red de Seguridad y Defensa de América Latina]. Guatemala endured a 36-year civil war, which ended in 1996 with the signing of peace accords" (1). In spite of peace accords, this widespread everyday violence persists and can be traced back to political instability: "Sustained political violence signifi-cantly contributes to the normalization of violence, as does the related inabil-ity of the state to provide legitimate institutional control of violence" (Winton, "Urban Violence" 168). These statistics about violence in Central America are what lie beneath the surface that is scratched by social media images and Edward's summation that "the government has lost control."

Chapter 1 discusses how many Central Americans who arrive in the US seeking refuge are criminalized as noncitizens, something rhetorician Jennifer Wingard explains is a part of a tradition of exclusion: "Throughout history, minority groups (e.g., women, Native Americans, immigrants) have been tar-geted in order to define US citizenship through negation" (48). This exclu-sion—as it manifests in performances of citizenship in the US and economic markets in the US and Central America—accounts for the violence Edward and other migrants describe as a part of their lived realities. This chapter examines the reasons many migrate from Central America, particularly Gua-temala, and offers a call to decolonize how immigration is framed and dis-cussed along neocolonial logic based in neocolonial laws that marginalize Indigenous populations with less power for business interests. In doing so, this chapter resists the sanitizing narrative that labels the systematic genocide of Indigenous Maya in Guatemala as a "civil war," rather than *la violencia* of a US-backed Guatemalan government. This despotic government damaged the social fabric of Indigenous communities through scorched-earth campaigns and the massacres of villages with gender-based sexual violence, all of which sowed the seeds of the current violence, fear, and distrust that motivate migration abroad.

IMPORTED VIOLENCE

The US support of the Guatemalan government as it waged its systematic genocide of the Indigenous Maya in the guise of a "civil war" should not be overlooked when considering the more recent surges of migrants from Central America (Sanford; Sittig and González; Torres; Ujpán). The "civil war" exacted an immense toll on human life and entire communities: "The second cycle of civil war peaked in 1983, when the Guatemalan army gained the upper hand. During this period the army admitted that it had destroyed more than 440 towns and villages. . . . It was estimated that from 1981 to 1983 between 500,000 and 1,500,000 were displaced internally or externally" (Ujpán 10). Of the 1.5 million displaced, the vast majority were Indigenous people who had already been living on a small portion of the agricultural land not sold off to transnational corporate interests. These Maya were part of a large population migrating to the US at that time who were reclassified by Reagan's administration as economic migrants rather than refugees seeking safety from human rights abuses (Gzesh).

The United States' support of Guatemala's government as a part of the United States' Cold War strategy against communism left a legacy of institutional instability and violence that continues to affect migration. The current violence benefits the business interests of transnational companies that possess the majority of agricultural land in Guatemala. During the final years of *la violencia* of the "civil war," Guatemala continued to rank as the worst in human rights violations: "The U.S.-based Council of Hemispheric Affairs named Guatemala as the worst human rights violator in Latin America for 1989, 1990, 1991, and 1992" (Green 67). Indigenous Guatemalan Ignacio Bizarro Ujpán narrates events during and directly after the "civil war" / *la violencia* in *Joseño: Another Mayan Voice Speaks from Guatemala*. Ujpán testifies to the heightened violence against Indigenous Maya: "There is much more violence in this year of 1990 than there was in previous years. Day after day there are more massacres of the naturales [Indians] of our beautiful Tzutuhil town. . . . Almost on a daily basis, the Tzutuhiles are killed by the bullets" (148). For audiences in the US who have difficulty identifying with the lives lost because of US intervention, it's important to consider how we look to

Latin America and the lives and towns lost to "the bullets" as reflections of the United States' own settler colonial past and wars against Indigenous people.

Another disturbing manifestation of violence that can also be traced to the post–"civil war" 1990s and something that continues in Guatemala today is the increased rate of femicide. Regarding recent increases of femicide, Obinna states that "in Guatemala, the number of women murdered each year has more than tripled since 2000 (England, 2018)" (807). In 2008 the Femicide Law was passed in Guatemala; however, before then "it was legal for men to rape their wives, and until 2006, if a man raped a woman or a girl over 12 he could avoid punishment if he married her" (Sanford 66).

While this was happening in Guatemala, there were similarly disturbing instances of femicide near the US-Mexico border, where many migrants seeking refuge from gender-based violence can arrive while attempting to cross to the US. The rhetorical activities of community activists in Ciudad Juárez have brought public attention to the murders of several hundred women, and Tricia Serviss analyzes why these deaths are often dismissed. Serviss explains that the victims themselves are often blamed by local reporters and government officials:

> Once the North American Free Trade Agreement (NAFTA) took effect in 1994, attention turned toward maquiladora workers, mainly women from Juárez and other parts of Mexico and Guatemala who migrated often with husbands and children in tow. These female workers, like other generations of migrant workers of Juárez before them, were often represented as transient, immoral, and the clear instigators of any violence directed towards them. (611)

The characterization of these murdered women as "transient, immoral," and "instigators" parallels the patterns of dehumanization the Guatemalan government and army practiced as they committed the genocide of the Indigenous Maya through the purposeful conflation of all Indigenous people as guerillas. Framing the violence as a "civil war" suggests mutual responsibility in spite of the systemic inequality. As Indigenous Guatemalan writer Ujpán observes, these murders continued after the "civil war," thereby provoking continued migration as a result of forced displacement.

Violence and threats of violence in Central America, primarily in Guatemala, contributed to the displacement of Indigenous Maya left with few options other than to migrate to the US. Because of the United States' colonial history, decolonial methodology provides the necessary framework for making sense of the senseless violence that comes as a result of neocolonialism and the exploitation of nonwhite labor. CRT scholar Eduardo Bonilla-Silva makes the connection between racism and colonialism when he explains "that racism emerged in modernity (16th century) when the logic and practice of race was used to justify colonization, land dispossession, genocide, and extreme labor exploitation" (1777). Latinx rhetoric scholar Ana Ribero furthers this claim in her explanation of how current immigration policy supports legacies of colonial power: "Serving the coloniality of power, immigration legislation guards the borders of citizenship by stipulating and policing the boundaries of illegality and working as neoliberal disciplinary systems for labor subordination through nationalist means" (Ribero, "Citizenship" 38). A decolonial approach to immigration is necessary for untangling migration from criminality and, instead, centering how US policy should seek to imagine a new world, by first redressing the outcomes of colonialism, in the form of military power and transnational business, while providing refuge for those impacted. Migrants can no longer be viewed as simply the cost of modernity and of doing transnational business.

The legacy of colonialism in Guatemala can be seen in the logic of violence and threats of violence that dictated the genocide and resulted in the land dispossession that forced Indigenous Guatemalans to seek refuge in the US. By the end of the scorched-earth campaign of the Guatemalan armies during the "civil war," "over 626 Maya villages had been burned to the ground" (Sanford 55). In this chapter a decolonial approach helps untangle the connections between the economies of violence in Central America and contemporary factors, prompting large numbers of migrants from Guatemala to come to the US leading up to and during my time at the Sanctuary (2013–16). Evidenced by the caravans through Mexico, migration from Guatemala continues in no small part because of increased levels of femicide and violence against young men and women (S. England; Obinna; Serviss). Because of the heightened level of awareness brought to Central American migrants with the politicization of the caravans by President Trump, the question remains as to why migrants continued coming despite US officials urging them to stay at home and discouraging them from migrating. This chapter addresses this question through a discussion of the violence inflicted on Guatemalan Maya during and following the "civil war" that the US backed in no small part because of transnational corporate interests. In this chapter I argue for a decolonial understanding of immigration, specifically for Indigenous Guatemalans whose communities and ways of life have forever been altered by the US, at the very least by turning a blind eye to the genocidal violence that resulted following intervention based on business interests. I make this argument in order to reframe the topos of immigration, centering the effects and the legacies of

68 · CHAPTER 3

colonialism on Indigenous people while decentering arguments grounded in US policies that protect white property and citizenship. Statistical data arrived at through surveys at the Sanctuary serves as a point of departure into these interrelated, and often tragic, factors.

DECOLONIZING THE PARTICIPANT OBSERVER ROLE AND LIMITATIONS

As a participatory observer from 2013 to 2016, I taught English language classes to adult students, primarily Indigenous Maya from Guatemala, taking short notes during breaks from class and writing much longer notes after class. When I first started this research, I made inquiries about the students' perspectives, experiences, and aspirations for their lives and the lives of their families. My research on issues of race, citizenship, and language builds on ethnographic work of rhetorical scholars such as Ralph Cintron and Juan Guerra, who researched the public spaces occupied by Latinxs, as well as the literacy practices in transnational communities. I held Cintron's example in mind, especially how he skillfully weaves connections between rhetorical study and anthropological ethnography by explaining how the descriptive nature of fieldwork parallels the work of epideictic rhetoric, which similarly deals with traditions and rituals. Cintron concludes that the rhetorical nature of examining public and private spaces "is rhetorical long before its text, its ethnographies and theoretical treaties, come into being because the cultural stuff that becomes a fieldnote is rhetorical, as is the fieldnote itself" (3). Cintron furthermore provides an important reminder about the work at the Sanctuary in his description of his research as "a collection of ways by which a variety of people created *respect under conditions of little or no respect*" (164). The issue of respect is something scholars practicing decolonial methodologies try to honor as they redress the dehumanization of "empirical" research that can operate exclusively within colonial logic and epistemology. Similarly, Juan Guerra's work teaching within migrant Mexicanos in Chicago laid important groundwork for research on literacy within marginalized communities. This book answers Guerra's call to "learn as much as we can about the actual lived experiences of members of marginalized groups in the United States, especially those whose limited economic and educational options give them little choice but to make their homes in highly segregated racial and ethnic communities out of which some members rarely venture" (5). Guerra is also quick to remind researchers that the goal is "to proliferate information about a culture rather than to appropriate it" (10). Heading northeast on the 880 freeway, I could not escape how the landscape would shift from residential suburban areas to more industrial urban spaces where the cars seemed to drive more erratically to a soundtrack of taco trucks blaring ranchero ballads from busy gas station parking lots with vendors selling hats and apparel for the local sports teams.

My friendship with Mateo, the missionary coordinating classes at the Sanctuary, also reinforced my level of respect for and commitment to volunteering at the Sanctuary in a participatory observer role. I was not merely coming into this vulnerable population's shared space and collecting data, but I was contributing my skills and labor to benefit their purpose for being there. An enduring criticism of how academics conduct research, especially with marginalized populations, is that these communities open themselves up to a unidirectional collection of stories, data, and observations without concern for how researchers could contribute to or work with the community. Indigenous scholar Linda Tuhiwai Smith advocates for research methods that contribute to the communities involved. Smith asserts that researchers need to consider the role of dignity when working with Indigenous communities: "To be able to share, to have something worth sharing, gives dignity to the giver. To accept a gift and to reciprocate gives dignity to the receiver" (105). Tuhiwai Smith's advocacy prioritizing dignity with Indigenous communities is particularly relevant in my research with Indigenous Maya students. Wanting to maintain this vulnerable population's sense of dignity can mean I do not use my position of authority as a teacher to probe for information as a researcher.

Because this Indigenous student population comes from a country with a history of "civil war" and current drug trafficking and high rates of gender-based violence, respect and dignity take precedence over any academic pretense of arriving at absolute certainty about the lives of this population. Traditional research methods like surveys and interviews were incorporated, but respect for the students' comfort level always came first. Decolonial practice can and often does incorporate existing research methods. However, Godwin Agboka makes the case that decolonial approaches ask for a reframing of relations between the researcher and those at the center of a study. He explains, "The underlying problem is that when research participants are seen as subjects, they become only objects to be exploited, rather than equal partners in the research process. It is no surprise that Boynton suggested that the term 'subjects' be banned from reports on humans, because it is demeaning and smacks of colonialism" (300). Because of my friendship with Mateo and my role as a teacher with the adult immigrant students, I never saw the students at the Sanctuary as "subjects." Instead, we were all a part of the ecology that operated from a shared spirit of volunteerism and the giving of one's time within a community that could benefit from what could be offered.

I recognize that my friendship with Mateo, currently spanning twenty-plus years, could be seen as a potential limitation; inherent bias could influence how I observed and interpreted the work at the Sanctuary. However, I believe my lengthy friendship with Mateo was a strength because of Mateo's long-standing role in this immigrant community; my goal as both a friend and a researcher was to protect this vulnerable population with whom I developed my own relationships as an educator. Not only did Mateo's friendship help establish trust with the adult student population, which was vulnerable because of immigration status and language ability, but our friendship also made me more accountable as a teacher and researcher in this community.

As a researcher I was also allowed access to survey data collected by Mateo for the benefit of his administration. Because Mateo's work is that of a missionary, the surveys included questions regarding religious affiliation, church membership, and prayer preferences. And while religious organizations like the Catholic Church have been synonymous with colonialism across the Americas, the Sanctuary is not a Catholic denomination. In terms of religious institutions and migrant dignity, rhetorician Anne Teresa Demo describes how a joint pastoral letter by US Catholic bishops and the Conferencia del Episcopado Mexicano helps reframe immigration debates when espousing an "approach to migrant dignity and sovereignty [that] established a moral framework that denationalizes the immigrant issue" (51). The denationalization of immigration is an important part of the process of decolonizing immigration epistemology and arguments grounded in the logic of coloniality. In the next section, some results from the surveys I circulated at the Sanctuary provide points of departure into issues of violence sanitized survey data cannot reveal because Guatemalan Maya come from a tradition of learned silence and contemporary violence minimized when concretized as numeric values.

SURVEY DATA AS A STARTING POINT

From 2013 to 2016, the Sanctuary's English program served somewhere between two hundred and three hundred students, the majority of them in the beginner class, with varying exposure to written literacy. Illiteracy for Indigenous Guatemalans had decreased dramatically since the 1940s; however, "at 44 percent of the population, it is still the highest rate in Central America" (Ujpán 12). In total at the Sanctuary, fifty-four surveys were collected at two times in 2014 and 2015, with thirty-eight male respondents and sixteen female respondents. While this number might not suggest a significant sample size, this number makes up about 15 to 20 percent of the students attending classes at the Sanctuary between September 2013 and June 2016. More importantly, this response represents a significant number and percentage for data collected because of the vulnerable populations who shared information related to immigration status. The parallel hauntings of this research are the desire to teach more students and collect more data while reconciling with the ephemeral nature of the informal education space where students could come and go with irregularity.

I started with surveys as a technology for inquiring about the students' perspectives on language, citizenship, and race to provoke more nuanced follow-up questions during informal interviews. Anonymous surveys provided a necessary first step in establishing the variety of perspectives in a given community, and the range of participation also seemed to indicate how much apprehension members of the community have in discussing certain topics. In addition, the willingness of those who participated demonstrated the amount of trust the students have in the program, church staff, Mateo, and me as the researcher. In a British study of 1,860 respondents in Guatemala, trust was identified as a key factor because of "high levels of distrust in state security and justice systems [that] exacerbated the widespread prevalence of perverse social organizations [gangs], and associated levels of fear" (McIlwaine and Moser 978). The silence I met to some questions and invitations to talk contributed to a constellation of factors that suggested a prevailing fear that endured. With a history of genocide by the Guatemalan government of Indigenous Maya, institutions with a legacy of colonialism remain understandably suspect or questionable for many Guatemalans.

On Monday evenings Isabel, the assistant to the pastor and administrator of the English program within the Sanctuary, always began with a short prayer session in the basement. Before the prayer session, Isabel would often circulate around the church, prompting more advanced and returning students to come downstairs, working against the passive resistance to attending, enacting strategies of silence, or the "'cultura de silencio' (law of silence)" used to avoid confrontation with authority (McIlwaine and Moser 972). In Guatemala silence and secrecy function as survival strategies: "The dual lessons of silence and secrecy were for me the most enlightening and disturbing. Silence about the present situation when talking with strangers is a survival strategy that Mayas have long utilized" (Green 68). Even though the Sanctuary church might seem its own community, fear and silence stemming from historical and current violence in Guatemala stay with many students who have

72 • CHAPTER 3

learned to distrust neighbors and authority out of necessity. Even at home in
Guatemala, researchers found a sense of trust and community limited: "It was
common for participants to report a sense of community only in their school,
block or amongst a particular set of neighbors or interest group" (Winton,
"Youth" 177). Out of a concern for safety, some students were understandably
not as forthcoming.

At the Sanctuary I taught beginner, intermediate, and advanced classes;
wrote letters of support for students; and attended meetings with staff, teachers, and students. I shared dinners with volunteer teachers, talked over
lunches with Mateo, attended some church celebrations and children's birthdays in East Bay apartments, and spoke with students from my classes over
countless cups of church coffee with pan dulce during class breaks. While the
survey data may have revealed that many of the students were males from
Guatemala, somewhere between the ages of eighteen to twenty-three or thirty
to thirty-five, who came to the US for job opportunities and because of the
threat of gangs back home, the whole story cannot be told by the data alone.
This particular age group would no doubt be particularly guarded because in
Guatemala "children born in the 1980s and 1990s witnessed firsthand the government invading their homes; torturing their parents, relatives, and neighbors; killing them; raping their mothers and sisters; and burning their homes,
livestock, and means of survival" (Sanford 55–56). In the following sections,
the violence discussed by the student Edward provokes further inquiry into
violence in Central America, specifically in Guatemala, as well as violence
against women that can be contextualized by survey data, offering some light
in the dark that is a culture of silence.

DISTRUSTING "CIVIL WAR"

The fear and distrust of Indigenous Guatemalan Maya, as well as their resulting silence, can be traced to the ways the Ladino-led Guatemalan army was
allowed by the government to torture and disappear potential subversives with
impunity during the thirty-six years of genocidal violence, referred to as "civil
war." The trauma of this violence inflicted upon many Indigenous people who
had members of their families killed was further compounded when they were
expected to live alongside the soldiers in military outposts who committed
these inhuman crimes. Researcher Victoria Sanford interviewed Guatemalan
women who allowed themselves to be sexually assaulted by soldiers during
the "civil war"; when Sanford inquired as to why these women might sub-
mit themselves to this abuse, "the response was always that they knew if they

did not go, the army would come to take their young daughters" (55). The realities of this "civil war" have been described as "the horror of living side by side with the person responsible for the murder of your father, or of walking by the innumerable clandestine cemeteries that scar the local landscape, or of remaining silent and fearful in the face of the half secrets of who did what to whom" (Green 10). What contributes to the sense of distrust was the army's conflation of guerillas with all Indigenous people as well as the torture inflicted within the army of those conscripted against their will. As a colonial apparatus, the army attempted to assimilate and erase the cultural identities of both Ladinos and Indigenous Maya who were forced to serve.

Fear and threats of violence and death were a way of life for those forced to join the Ladino-led Guatemalan army. In an interview, a former member of the army explains how he was tortured by military superiors while serving, with very few options to leave. In *The Mayans among Us,* the former soldier explains how his choice was either to join or become a target of guerilla fighters: "They'd say, 'Do you want to die, or are you going to become a member of the guerilla?' And so what the army did was make a person disappear, because the truth was that one was a source of information for the guerilla. So, it was a situation with no way out" (Sittig and González 39). The Maya forced to join the army come back fundamentally changed: "As one villager noted, 'They leave as Indians, but they don't come back Indian'" (Green 64). In the army the soldiers were taught to hate everyone, even themselves, as a part of a systematic dehumanization of Indigenous men who chose to join and those who were able to avoid enlisting. Joining the army assimilated Indigenous Maya into a Ladino ideology that internalized racism. At the same time, the former Guatemalan soldier highlights how the guerillas followed a similar pattern of logic based on violence and threats of violence that made the soldiers untrusting and hateful.

While soldiers in the army made individual decisions and felt a lack of choices, the genocidal scorched-earth campaigns of the army that massacred entire villages cannot be ignored because they bring to bear unspeakable human rights violations. As described in a human rights report, a massacre in the village of Dos Erres highlights the army's brutality and complete lack of regard for human life: "People were 'disappeared,' tortured, mutilated, burned alive, or forced to join the military. Children were thrown against walls or into pits and covered with dead adult bodies to kill them" (Sitting and González 43). The horrific tragedies and violations of human rights during the "civil war" are such that the culture of silence practiced by some Indigenous Guatemalans can be understood as a response to trauma inflicted on generations of Indigenous Guatemalans and passed on for survival. In the next section,

74 • CHAPTER 3

violence against women and femicide are closely examined because sexual violence has long been a strategy of colonial power, supported by a patriarchal ideology that dehumanizes women, and the normalizing of said violence continues to cause many women to migrate from Guatemala.

VIOLENCE AGAINST WOMEN

In the surveys I circulated and collected at the Sanctuary, the largest population of people surveyed were men ages eighteen to twenty-nine, totaling twenty. From all the surveys collected at the Sanctuary, the largest number of both genders was in their twenties, totaling 45 percent of all males and 50 percent of all females. The high percentage of work-age women from Central America alludes to the different motivations to come to the US from Latin American countries. Research on femicide in Central America points out that Guatemalan women in their twenties were the most at risk of being victims: "The highest cohort of female victims is aged between 25 and 29 years at 16.3% of the femicides reported" (Obinna 820). That 50 percent of the women taking classes at the Sanctuary were in their twenties could be explained by the highest rates of being at risk of femicide. In the space of the Sanctuary, the profound nature of these threats and realities experienced by the women in the classes might account for why the men and women would often segregate from one another during breaks, drinking coffee and eating pan dulce at lunch tables with those of the same gender. The realities of these high rates of gender-based violence might also account for why some of the higher-performing female students were reluctant to move into higher-level classes that were predominantly male.

Historically, women in Guatemala endured all manner of terrorism, with their husbands and sons "disappearing" at the hands of the army or conscripted to serve and take part in the scorched-earth campaigns against other Indigenous villages. Citing the same human rights report that detailed the massacre in the village of Dos Erres, Sittig and González describe how sexual violence and violence against women were systemic during the massacre: "Miscarriages were provoked, fetuses cut from wombs, and women were systematically raped before they were killed" (43). Since the end of *la violencia*, women in Guatemala face the alarming reality of the number of women murdered tripling since 2000 (S. England; Obinna). These shocking details and statistics underscore the need for new worlds and new realities. Decolonizing immigration and rethinking the reality complicitly agreed upon through cyclical returns to the status quo are necessary to address femicide and sexual violence because it is the colonial logic of violence that seeks to fracture and erase cultures through these particular forms of violence.

The sexual violence described in this scholarship provides important information I did not ask about in the surveys and informal interviews I conducted at the Sanctuary. As a part of my role as volunteer teacher, I wanted to practice the respect of treating the students as humans rather than research subjects, something decolonial researchers agree is often the least researchers can do. I additionally did not want to take advantage of my authority as a teacher, especially when many of the survey responses seemed to avoid overt discussion of violence. Historically, Guatemalan women have had to avoid men in positions of authority for their own safety because "during the war, army soldiers and other security officers were responsible for 94.3 percent of all sexual violence against women" (Sanford 55). Still, the violence described heretofore is not disconnected from the lived reality of the migrants at the Sanctuary. In an interview with a reporter for the *Los Angeles Times,* a Central American woman taking part in a Christmas ceremony at the church I call the Sanctuary recounts the violence in Central America that warrants a content warning because of its viciousness. The *Times* reporter writes:

> Guadalupe, 37, who asked that her last name be withheld, is among a family of 11—six of them between ages 3 and 15—who fled a San Salvador suburb earlier this year. She wept as she told their story: Her sister and brother-in-law were extorted by gang members. When they could no longer pay, he was pressed to become a drug courier and refused. He and his 12-year-old son were then driven a short distance from the home and shot to death. Gang members next demanded $15,000 from Guadalupe and her husband, who operated a small grocery store. When they could not pay, she was pulled off a city bus, she recounted, beaten and sexually assaulted in a sugar cane field as her 3-year-old daughter watched. (Romney)

Tragically, the current drug and gang violence described by Guadalupe taking place in El Salvador follows the same pattern of violence and femicide Guatemalan women experience currently. In her 2023 book *Textures of Terror: The Murder of Claudina Isabel Velasquez and Her Father's Quest for Justice,* Victoria Sanford documents high rates of violence against women in Guatemala, where women are treated like property, finding that "90 percent of victims of intrafamilial violence are women and girls," making the case that intrafamilial violence was gender-based violence (59). This current normalization of gender-based violence continues in a tradition that can be traced back to the "civil war," where "violence against women took many forms during the counterinsurgency war . . . [;] pregnant women eviscerated, their unborn babies used as balls to play with; women forced to cook for the soldiers after having watched their husbands tortured and killed" (Green 31). The gender-based violence within families and by gangs can be understood as having been normalized during the genocidal *violencia,* when women were expected to suffer these violations without being allowed to process these assaults or prosecute those who committed these human rights atrocities.

The trauma suffered within these communities not only disrupts the social fabric of the culture but contributes to the internalized distrust of authority that warrants a culture of silence. Linda Green explains that the "widespread use of rape during counterinsurgency war was a gendered way in which the military attacked the social fabric of family and community life" (32). This legacy of violence can be traced to colonialism because "fear and oppression have been the dual and constant features of Guatemalan history since the arrival of Pedro Alvarado and his conquistadores in the early sixteenth century" (Green 64). Colonial logics of immigration are ill-suited to redress the violence against women and femicide in Central America because it is the colonial logic of violence that rationalizes these violations in an attempt to erase any possibility of a different reality.

The ethical frameworks with which we discuss immigration need to be reimagined because they are the very same that discount gender-based violence or readily accept it as something someone seeking refuge, or a better life for their family, deserves. In an examination of the frequently crossed northern Mexican border town of Ciudad Juárez, femicide continued to be widespread in areas impacted by neocolonial transnational corporations. Researcher Tricia Serviss concludes that these deaths are rationalized and accepted as the cost of transnational business: "Women killed by femicide were cast as casualties of the transnationalization of Juárez" (612). Within the dominant understandings of immigration, the potential for beatings, sexual assault, and the death of migrants is a risk put on the migrants despite the resulting value of their cheap labor. Latinx rhetorician Sonia Arellano describes the sexual violence many migrant women risk on their journey to the US:

> Women decide to migrate because they don't have any family in their home country and/or their lives are at risk in their home country . . . [;] they are often traveling alone or with children. Many smugglers, bandits, coyotes, brothel owners, and law enforcement officials that women migrants encounter are men who take advantage of women traveling alone by charging them more to cross, robbing and raping them, kidnapping them for ransom, coercing them into sex work, and negotiating sex to avoid legal ramifications

or raping them while in law enforcement custody. For women, sexual assault on this journey is considered inevitable. (508)

What Arellano describes as the inevitability of sexual assault during migration parallels trends in reported data: "In a 2017 Médecins Sans Frontières (MSF) report, nearly a third of the women who entered Mexico on the journey northward reported being sexually abused" (Obinna 807). Given this high possibility for experiencing some form of gender-based violence, it is important to remember the fear and threats of violence if these migrant women remain at home. Obinna provides a succinct reminder of the reasons why so many migrate: "The staggering rate of femicide, rape, and forced recruitment of females to be girlfriends of gang members (novias de pandilleros) has produced patterns of behavior that directly influence women's decisions to migrate" (807). Decolonizing immigration could unlink the patriarchal approach to policy regarding gender-based violence and women's bodies that somehow rationalizes this logic of violence for which there has been little to no culpability. In the US, if we want to evaluate where we stand in terms of our culpability for the violence perpetuated in border countries and transnational business interests, we cannot continue to turn a blind eye to the reality our policy imposes.

GANG AND NARCO VIOLENCE

As mentioned earlier, the largest population of men at the Sanctuary were those ages eighteen to twenty-nine. When considering reasons younger men immigrate from Guatemala, the violence in cities like the capital city of Guatemala City inflicted by mara street gangs needs to be considered, as it is a reason women migrate—to avoid being forced to be a "girlfriend"—and because young men are threatened to join or are subjected to assaults. In an article studying the geography of violence in Guatemala City, there were estimates of between 53 and 330 different mara street gangs. When surveying younger men, the researcher also found that "older age groups and young men . . . described the constant struggle of maintaining enough distance from the maras not to get drawn in" (Winton, "Youth" 176). Additionally, research shows that not only were young men afraid of becoming drawn in by the gangs, but younger people in general also experienced distrust from within their communities because of their age. Winton explains that "the majority of participants reported an acute lack of trust of young people by older members of the community, with young people excluded and stigmatized by association" ("Youth"

78 • CHAPTER 3

179). With concerns about being entangled with one of the many gangs, young men might feel less likely to stay in their country because they feel excluded by older adults in their communities.

In a *Los Angeles Times* article about the Sanctuary and other churches offering sanctuary, a young migrant spoke about the violence and pressure from gangs. The *Times* author describes "Rene, who, fearing for his safety, asked that only his middle name be used. The 14-year-old Mayan youth said he had been beaten by gang members who were pressuring him to join" (Romney). In response to one of my surveys at the Sanctuary, gang violence was chosen by 20 percent of respondents as their reason for migrating, with the fewest answering "family in the US"; however, 20 percent also responded that they "preferred not to answer." The preference not to answer suggests more of the fear related to the violence that is better left unsaid. Even though the percentages were similar in the ages of the adult students, the number of men responding to the survey was twice the number of women. These high numbers of young men also speak to the absence of men in Central American countries where gangs have a stronghold and force membership at a young age. In the same research on gang violence in Guatemala City, there is a sense of hopelessness many feel as a result of gang violence: "One 17-year-old young woman in Guatemala City noted that: 'There will be more people involved in gangs, more deaths. This is going to increase here. There's not much hope'" (Winton, "Youth" 171). Migrating to the US is an act of the hopeful and an indication of the potential for a better world.

However, even Indigenous people living outside of cities also live in fear of gang and cartel violence. Journalist Óscar Martínez describes the violence occurring on plantation land owned by narco-traffickers and shared with transnational companies. Martínez describes violence on par with that of *la violencia*:

> In May of 2011, on a plantation called Los Cocos, in an unpopulated stretch of land across La Libertad, there was a massacre of twenty-seven people. According to official reports, the perpetrators were Los Zetas. Their target was the plantation owner, but apparently they couldn't find him and they took out their revenge on the campesinos instead. Some were decapitated with chainsaws. An investigator showed me a picture of the bodies still wearing their heavy work boots. (*History* 73)

The massacre of twenty-seven Indigenous campesinos echoes the genocidal scorched-earth tactics of *la violencia,* though narco-violence is purely in the name of capitalism. Because the cause of this massacre was a struggle over access to drug routes along the plantation land, this violence can be viewed as a war over a neocolonial market share with Indigenous lives reduced to disposable labor.

CRIMINALIZATION IN THE US

All of this discussion of violence tends to be interpreted through the commercial media that sensationalizes the violence at the cost of the victims. Toward the end of my time at the Sanctuary, Trump promised, as part of his 2016 election campaign, to deport "at least two million," so campuses and cities across the country responded by declaring themselves sanctuaries, vowing to protect undocumented students and not aid federal immigration enforcement (Wang). The certainty with which migrants spoke about the security of living in California wavered, as it did for many undocumented people who once believed in working toward their chance at a better life.

While a presidential candidate, Trump made campaign promises that appealed to the xenophobic and nationalist ideology of many who would vote for him. However, President Barack Obama's history with immigration remained something of a campaign promise deferred. Ana Ribero decodes what Obama said about "prioritizing the deportation of 'criminal aliens'"; she explains that instead of targeting drug and gang-related offenses, "in actuality Obama's policy prioritizes the detention and deportation of migrants who may have no criminal record other than their deportation. . . . Their criminalization denies them the ability to ever adjust their legal status" (Ribero, "Citizenship" 38). President Obama perpetuated neocolonial logic that erased paths to citizenship for those who had already been detained because they no doubt had lives and children in the US that they wanted to return to.

With high rates of homicide and low trust in law enforcement, the inner-city crime of the East Bay and living with the threat of deportation seem less severe than the insecurity and reality of violence in migrants' home countries. According to the International Organization for Migration, deportation rates increased in 2011, when "the US forcibly returned 30,855 Guatemalans to their country by air. This was the highest number of direct returns in five years. Mexico sent another 31,427. . . . Those 62,282 returnees represent approximately 12 percent of the irregular Guatemalan population living in the US" (D. Field). Low-income Latinxs in the US also experienced the trauma related to raids where houses were searched, with young children learning distrust of law enforcement: "Their first-hand observations involved witnessing their parents, grandparents, and other family elders humiliated and treated as criminals"

(M. Romero 31). In my exchanges with and surveys of my Guatemalan Indigenous students, I sought to refrain from posing probing questions that might needlessly ask someone to relive trauma. Even with the threat of deportation, many Central American migrants seek refuge from violence as their definition of a better life in the US. Literacy and Latinx rhetoric scholar Steven Alvarez identifies the Spanish term *superarse* that captures the idea of the better life many migrate for: "Superarse and the corresponding noun superación mean to overcome barriers, to move up—literally, to surpass one's current state" (*Brokering* xvi). According to Ana Arana's research for *Foreign Affairs,* many of the men and women who come to the US to improve the lives of their families find that when their children rejoin them in the US, their children "have already been recruited by the maras [gangs] in the rough neighborhoods where they grew up" (104). Many who migrate attempt to *superarse,* although violence continues to impact the next generation who are left behind with their own barriers.

MIGRATION ON FILM

Guatemala's labeling of its Indigenous people as so-called narcos performs the same rhetorical strategy as Trump's vilifying the migrant caravans coming up from Central America as MS-13 gang members. The appeal to fear of Mara Salvatrucha, MS-13, can be traced to the high rates of violence and homicide in Guatemala, El Salvador, and Honduras; however, Trump's appeal to fear purposely conflates all migrants with MS-13, just as the Guatemalan government conflated all Indigenous people with guerillas. A 2009 US film produced about the process of immigrating to the US from Central America called *Sin Nombre* remains relatively unfamiliar to many in the US who question the reasons large numbers of people from Central America migrate. Cary Fukunaga's film depicts the omnipresence of MS-13 gangs that leads to fear that is "more temporally constant for young men" (Winton, "Youth" 176). Wider viewing and recognition of *Sin Nombre* could help audiences of voters in the US better understand the threat of violence many in Central America live with and why many risk assaults, robbery, sexual assaults, and even death on the journey north to the US.

Sin Nombre centers around Sayra, a teenager from Honduras, and Willy, a Mexican MS-13 member. Sayra is migrating to the US with her uncle and father when their path crosses with that of Willy, whose girlfriend was recently killed by the leader of his gang, Lil' Mago. Sayra and her family are riding atop of *la bestia,* or the beast, a train many migrants ride on top of on their journey through Mexico to the US, when Willy, Lil' Mago, and other members of their

MS-13 gang begin robbing migrants riding on top of the train. Latin American studies scholar Yajaira Padilla describes the gendered dynamic of Lil' Mago's attempted sexual assault of Sayra:

> Lil' Mago discovers Sayra huddled under a tarp with her father and uncle.... During this scene, high-angle shots are used to mark the gendered relations of power between Lil' Mago and Sayra, and by extension, the other terrorized undocumented migrants that surround her as they too are prey for the Mara Salvatrucha.... If not for the intervention of Willy, who kills Lil' Mago in an act of revenge for another crime, Sayra would have been subjected to the same fate that countless other female migrants have suffered: rape and even death. (162–63)

While films are the fictional vision of filmmakers, the Sanctuary's English program coordinator, Mateo, told me he's had migrants tell him that *Sin Nombre* was the most accurate depiction of what their experiences of coming to the US were like.

While the attempted sexual assault that *Sin Nombre* depicts during the life-threatening journey to the US can be blamed on the actions of gang members, Sonia Arellano argues that the sexual violence that many migrant women experience is state-sanctioned. Arellano explains that governmental awareness without action makes them complicit: "Both the US and Mexican governments know about the violences women experience, yet the governments take no action, and sexual violences continue to be an integral part of migrants' journey north" (502). Like Arellano, I have spoken while on a Jesuit immersion trip to the US-Mexico border with migrant women who recounted their experiences with sexual violence. One woman explained to me that it did not happen in Mexico, but at the hands of a US Border Patrol officer when she was apprehended near Ciudad Juárez. This parallels the experience of many women in Guatemala who have reported their assaults to police because "a European Union survey showed that the police had raped more than a third of women who went to them to report a crime" (Sanford 79). Much like Arellano, I saw limitations as a researcher to do much more for this woman than bear witness to her experience. Arellano skillfully describes these unsettling limitations: "I will not know for myself the violences migrant women experience, and as a researcher, I will not come to some final 'truth' or answer in examining violences against migrant women. I hope researchers see value in what we can glean from this limitation but also understand that it is only a small part of a larger, material consequence" (507). The woman I spoke with on the Jesuit immersion trip wanted to share her story because she knows

82 · CHAPTER 3

how the mistreatment of migrants can happen due to the lack of awareness around these issues.

While there is often little that can be said or done when told of the inhumanity experienced by migrants, rhetorically listening and sharing the dehumanization of an economy of exclusion will hopefully bring into focus the criticism of an unbridled market and its effects on immigration and land displacement. Additionally, the decolonial practice of centering relations helps us as researchers to maintain the dignity of the people we interview and to make ethical considerations about the stories we hear.

CONCLUSION

"This violence [on social media]" Sanctuary student Edward said, "does not happen in the small town in El Salvador where I am from. In the bigger cities, yes. There, everyone knows people who are affected." From the standpoint of the US, it might be easier to rationalize that many of these deaths are related to people choosing to become involved in drug trafficking. However, journalists covering crime in Central America point out how violence includes people outside of the narcos: "According to the government, the 18th Street gang was targeting bus drivers and passing out fliers telling bus lines not to run or they risked paying a high price. At least eight drivers and transportation workers were killed in a 48-hour period" (Raney). Gang violence spans out beyond drug trafficking and applies the intimidation aspect to the extortion of public transportation. When I asked Edward how many people he knew who have been affected, he said, "Maybe fifteen."

Edward says the East Bay is not bad. He's been here since 1997. He said, "Nothing bad has happened in that time." Still, crime statistics about the East Bay report fluctuations of drug-related crime and robberies. In 2008 the Urban Strategies Council reported that the East Bay has some of the least safe areas, with the murder of African American men significantly higher than in other cities (Spiker et al.). Interest convergence in CRT reminds us that until African American men are safe, no one should feel safe.

"I tell my children," Edward said, "who were born here, to be safe and not to talk to strangers." He mentioned one of the dangerous streets in the East Bay, a street locals tell me was renamed at some point because the negative associations with crime haunted the former name of the street. He again said, "It's not that bad." In comparison to homicide statistics in Guatemala, Honduras, and El Salvador, the situation in the East Bay city where the Sanctuary was located might not seem "that bad."

In the next chapter, the struggle for the lease at the Sanctuary provides a metonymy for displacement and how language difference can be leveraged as a racial difference against nonwhites for the protection of white property. The English-speaking church is tacitly coded as white because the power of citizenship has always been associated with property rights, positioning the Spanish-speaking church on the same property as a nonwhite Other. As educators seeking to equip students with literacy skills, we are affected by the implications of racial, ethnic, and citizenship-related discrimination that lurk at the edges of what we do and impact what we are able to change.

CHAPTER 4

Sanctuary Struggle, Linguistic Discrimination, and Indigenous Displacement

INTRODUCTION

In January 2015 Mateo emailed the volunteer teachers at the Sanctuary's English program asking if we could write letters of support for the Spanish-speaking church that we could send to the governing body of the church's denomination. Pastor Pablo's Spanish-speaking church and congregation shared its location with a predominantly white, English-speaking church of the same denomination (see figure 1), operated by another pastor with a separate English-speaking congregation. Mateo explained to me that "the English-speaking church that shares the same property [as the Sanctuary] had recently re-signed the lease on the lot without co-signing with Pastor Pablo or anyone from the [Sanctuary] church."

Mateo added, "Pastor Pablo, his staff, and members of the congregation are concerned that the English-speaking church could evict them and take over the building for their own use." It was somewhat unclear who owned the property, but the English-speaking church signed the lease for the property that both the English-speaking church and the Spanish-speaking Sanctuary church shared. The Spanish-speaking church was appealing to the shared governing body in an attempt to get reassurance from the English-speaking church about the lease. The Spanish-speaking Sanctuary church felt they were left without rights and in a vulnerable position; this seemingly innocuous act

FIGURE 1. Entrance to the Sanctuary church on the left, with the rooftop of the English-speaking church building visible on the right.

of signing a lease is representative of the everydayness of racial discrimination and gentrification, which grabs land and displaces marginalized populations through the unseen violence of bureaucratic recordkeeping. Everyday racism is a part of the "inequitable conditions," such as the removal of the Spanish-speaking congregation from a lease, that "occur in covert ways, e.g., systemically at the policy level as well as in overt acts of racism" (Liggett 115). Though the signing of a lease might not seem like an overt act of discrimination, critical race theory reminds us how these seemingly "natural" or "neutral" acts can conceal injustices. At the same time, CRT scholars have long identified how laws protect white property and how whiteness itself functions as a form of property: "Whiteness and property share a common premise—a conceptual nucleus—of a right to exclude. This conceptual nucleus has proven to be a powerful center around which whiteness as property has taken shape" (Harris 1713). The English-speaking congregation aligns itself with whiteness as a property because the members are predominantly white, which also facilitates the colonial practice of assuming ownership of land.

Because language has the power "to name, institute, and enforce dominant white ideologies," immigration scholar Claudia Anguiano warns "against assuming that all the power subsists in the communicative impact of racist discourses" (100). The struggle over the Sanctuary lease is grounded in modernist ontologies that rely on "relentless growth and hyperaccumulation" that contributes to pilfering of resources in countries including Guatemala "with the expansion of oil palm cultivation, large-scale hydroelectric dams, mining for gold and strategic minerals" that results in "forced displacement, if not outright destruction, or particular territories" (Escobar xxxi). In one of the most expensive areas in the US, real estate remains one of the most valuable resources that can provoke legal struggle, especially when the act of aggression is little more than a signature on a piece of paper.

During the latter half of my time at the Sanctuary, the English-speaking congregation was mostly absent on the evenings when the volunteer teachers and adult students were present. Still, a feeling of uncertainty hung over the Sanctuary staff, casting doubts about the possibilities for the future. As a part of the Monday evening prayer sessions before class, Isabel would ask the students to pray for a positive resolution. Unfortunately, the communication between the churches demonstrated discrimination based on linguistic ability, or what has been called "linguicism," against the Spanish-speaking congregation, which, "like racial discourse—is similarly reflective and constitutive of power and underlying power relationships that are normalized in the broader social context and implied as the 'natural' order of things" (Liggett 114). Critical race theory helps in defining linguistic racism, which April Baker-Bell describes "as any system or practice of discrimination, segregation, persecution, or mistreatment of language based on membership in a race or ethnic group"; she goes on to say that "it is so normal that it is difficult to address because it is not acknowledged as a form of racism" (16). Literacy scholar Steven Alvarez makes the point that many multilingual migrants from Latin America, who speak Spanish and Indigenous languages, are familiar with being "discriminated against by Americans for [their] supposed illiteracy" in addition to experiencing discrimination from people with Latinx heritage (*Brokering* 91). The inquiries of the Spanish-speaking Sanctuary congregation about the lease could be ignored by the English-speaking congregation and governing body because the power difference of their language ability has been normalized through their exclusion from the lease, a move that also paralleled the colonizing practice of displacement.

The intersection of language and the leveraging of power at the Sanctuary can be traced to xenophobic ideology that underscores how policies such as "English only" never seek to improve communication but instead reify white nationalist rhetoric through the logic of colonizing monolingual ideology. The situation of the Sanctuary, lacking in institutional power, highlights the privilege given to dual-immersion language programs in affluent school districts in comparison to schools that have needed bilingual education and where it was outlawed. It mirrors the reality that English education researchers have observed: "Through a Western scholarly lens, monolingualism is routinely accepted as the norm, and bilingualism is accepted only as double monolingualism" (O. García 141). Conservative policymakers and media perpetuate monolingual ideologies with their rhetorical commonplaces about "bad" immigrants, including such arguments as "They don't learn the language," "They can't speak English right," or "They don't want to learn the language." These arguments are built on a faulty premise that ignores the fact that many migrants are already multilingual. These arguments "name, institute, and enforce dominant white ideologies" in support of English monolingualism; immigration scholar Claudia Anguiano reminds us that not "all the power subsists in the communicative impact of racist discourses" but is also communicated through seemingly innocuous policy about language (100). This chapter critically examines monolingual ideology that discriminates by using the English language to exclude and, in the case of the Sanctuary, manipulate access to property in the US, which further perpetuates the colonial role of churches and enacts the neocolonial land disposition against the Indigenous Maya migrant student population.

Tensions between the Spanish-speaking Sanctuary and the predominantly white, English-speaking church that share the same property provide a metonymy, or part for the whole, for gentrification. Gentrification as a neocolonial project shares many similarities with the land displacement experienced by many Indigenous Guatemalan migrants because the end goal in both cases is economic gain. After having been forced from their home countries, either through economic need or explicit violence, the Indigenous Guatemalan members of the congregation and English program continue to experience the displacement perpetuated by gentrification. Decolonial theory grounded in Indigenous epistemology foregrounds the centrality of Indigenous relationships with land. Indigenous rhetoric scholar Andrea Riley Mukavetz explains how maintaining space is a decolonial goal: "Within decolonial frameworks, the ultimate goal is to create, sustain, and maintain a habitable space for present and future generations—practicing decolonial theory is a form of care and love for ancestors and relatives" (126). The struggle over the lease at the Sanctuary follows a decolonial framework that seeks to maintain a space for gathering, worship, and learning. As this place is a colonial ideological apparatus, reimagining this space through a decolonial approach asks that we imagine realities that are not yet possible. At the same time, critical race theory

88 • CHAPTER 4

provides a particularly necessary framework for the case of the Sanctuary because these methodologies examine how policy protects property for white citizens, which is undergirded by racial and linguistic hierarchies.

This chapter examines how language was used to threaten to displace the Spanish-speaking congregation of the Sanctuary from their right to a shared property and presents data gathered from the migrant students at the Spanish-speaking church. These data and the critical race theory framework offer evidence that suggests monolingual arguments about migrants ignore the multiple linguistic literacies as a strategy of exclusion that upholds existing myths of white, monolingual supremacy. Survey and interview data reveal how many of the migrant students already speak their Indigenous Mayan language of Mam, in addition to the colonial language of Spanish, before seeking out opportunities to learn English in the US. I begin with the participant-observer experience of writing a letter to advocate for the Spanish-speaking church to provide additional context, which highlights how English continues to be the language of power and exclusion in the US. In the case of the Sanctuary, the power of English underscores how nonwhites are targeted by monolingual practices undergirded by legislation that ignores the communicative resources of multilingual practices. Through a mixed decolonial and critical race theory approach, this chapter examines the intersection of language discrimination and neocolonial land displacement as exclusion from a property lease and being forcibly moved from land in Guatemala.

A DIVIDED MISSION

On behalf of the Sanctuary's Spanish-speaking congregation, Mateo reached out to the teachers to write letters of support because our voices—in English—were less likely to be ignored. Even the Sanctuary staff were not heard; for example, Isabel, who served as an administrator, helped clean the church, organized church events, and was an impassioned, dedicated figure within the Sanctuary community, had been ignored. Writing studies scholars advocating for more inclusive approaches to language difference identify the phenomenon of dismissing speakers of nondominant varieties of English. Their ideas about nonstandard speakers of English being dismissed can be traced to beliefs that nonstandard varieties of English are considered inferior due, in part, to "the common, though inaccurate, view that varieties of English other than those recognized as 'standard' are defective" (Horner et al. 304). As someone who teaches academic writing, I told Mateo I would write a letter, hoping that whatever cultural capital or ethos I could channel as a professor at a local university would be conveyed in my request for support. Before drafting a letter, I looked at the organization's website so I could appeal to the potential reader overseeing the issue, according to the goals of the organization.

A couple days later, a thoughtful email was sent in response to my emailed letter. In the response the reverend explained that the organization wanted to support both churches in their work, but that any kind of imposed coordination would not be possible. The reverend described the churches as being "far from together in the work of the gospel." This phrase seemed to allude to a longer history of struggle between the two churches and congregations, which offered church services in two different languages while occupying the same property. Pastor Pablo of the Spanish-speaking church could speak English as well as Spanish, so the unwillingness of the English-speaking congregation to work together seemed to go beyond language.

Although the reverend at the governing body said no action would be taken, he at least felt pressure to respond. Following the letter writing, Mateo told me, "There's a meeting at the main church that oversees the denominations in the area. Members of the church are planning to go. If you have time, I'd welcome you to come."

The other volunteer teachers were also encouraged to attend. The aim was to discuss and raise concerns or objections about what had happened to the governing body of the local denominations. I felt somewhat guilty that I was unable to attend, but Mateo later relieved me of my guilt with his report of what happened during the meeting. He explained what happened, or, rather, what was not allowed to take place.

"Some members of the church were able to attend," he said, but there were no affordances made for the Spanish speakers in attendance (the Sanctuary had headsets for a translator when English speakers addressed the congregation). "The meeting proceeded in English. Even those who could speak some level of English had a difficult time understanding what was happening during the meeting, and there was no time given for anyone to ask questions." Members of the Sanctuary were excluded through linguicism, which is a "permanent fixture of life for English language learners who routinely encounter discrimination based on language proficiency and accent" (Liggett 115). This form of linguistic discrimination is much less overt in its everydayness compared with a less subtle policy like "English only"; however, the effects of linguicism still serve to support white supremacist ideology that affirms the naturalness of discrimination. The exclusion of the Spanish-speaking congregation from the property's lease was an unfortunate material outcome of the power of language to deny access by those in power. Language was at the root of the English-speaking church's ability to gain control of the lease with the

90 • CHAPTER 4

Sanctuary as cosigners of the lease, which also followed the historical role of churches to impose ideology over a space where land was stolen through the occupation of missions and the enslavement of Native people.

LANGUAGE DISCRIMINATION FOR LAND

The issue of land displacement and its intersection with language serves as the central point of contention in the struggle between the Spanish-speaking congregation and the English-speaking congregation on the shared property. Unfortunately for the Indigenous Maya from Guatemala, there is a history of language used to discriminate for the purpose of stealing land from Indigenous populations. For audiences familiar with *I, Rigoberta Menchú*, the roots of the genocide of the Guatemalan Maya can be traced back to wealthy Ladino landowners connected with transnational businesses attempting to displace Menchú's family and the Indigenous community from their lands. Menchú describes the cycle of struggle for land:

> My father fought for twenty-two years, waging a heroic struggle against the landowners who wanted to take our land and our neighbors' land. After many years of hard work, when our small bit of land began yielding harvests and our people had a large area under cultivation, the big landowners appeared. . . . Five of them [the Brols family] lived on a *finca* (farm) they had taken over by forcibly throwing the Indians of the region off their land. (103)

The story Menchú tells is one of genocide and displacement, even though this period of history is often characterized as "civil war" (Sanford; Torres). Menchú explains how, in reality, the Indigenous people were trying to keep their lands while being forced into military service, from which there was no escape because "in Guatemala if it has to do with the Government, there's no way we can defend ourselves" (103). Menchú clearly reminds us that in Guatemala, the government is somewhat synonymous with Ladinos, the mestizos who speak Spanish and trace their heritage back to Spain, thereby aligning power with the legacy of coloniality. Researchers in Guatemala similarly espouse Menchú's fatalistic description of struggles over land: "When people began to make demands that challenged local ladino power, particularly over land ownership, these confrontations ended in violence" (Green 45). In the translator's introduction to *I, Rigoberta Menchú*, the translator brings up the role of language in Menchú's struggle to raise awareness about the violence brought against the Maya in Guatemala. The translator explains that Menchú's

STRUGGLE, DISCRIMINATION, AND DISPLACEMENT · 91

use of Spanish was "learn[ing] the language of her oppressors in order to use it against them," noting that "Spanish was a language which was forced upon her" (Menchú xii). Spanish is in fact the language of the Ladino Guatemalan government and military, against whom Menchú and many Indigenous people struggled just to survive.

About the same time as the Sanctuary was going through its struggle with the lease, wealthy Silicon Valley leaders were devising ways to centralize their wealth and protect their property through proposed legislation. In 2014 Silicon Valley venture capitalist Tim Draper spearheaded legislation to propose splitting California into six separate states under the guise of creating economic accountability. However, critics identified Draper's agenda of turning Silicon Valley into a state that retains its tax wealth, separated from the less wealthy proposed states such as the Central Valley. The initiative failed to become a ballot measure due to a lack of signatures, but bipartisan opponents to the initiative "accused Draper of simply wanting to keep the tax wealth of Silicon Valley" (D. Romero). While this proposed legislation eventually failed, it still speaks to what CRT and decolonial scholars argue about white settler colonialism and its entitlement to what was once Indigenous land and the maintenance of property through policy that excludes nonwhites. While Silicon Valley venture capitalists like Draper might argue that the legislation has more to do with economic concerns than racial concerns, Derrick Bell long ago traced the root of laws regarding the protection of property to slavery. Bell makes the case that the Constitution was written with the idea in mind that "property in slaves should not be exposed to danger under a government instituted for the protection of property" ("Brown . . . Forty-Five Years" 175). That the Sanctuary is located in the East Bay of Northern California is complicated because the Bay Area is often regarded as a homogenous liberal utopia; however, gentrification and the development of previously undesirable areas of the Bay Area resurrect the spirit of Manifest Destiny, and white settlers feel entitled to land as property without considering how this land has been stolen from Native communities or how it might become a necessary aspect of reparations for the Black communities already inhabiting them.

At the Sanctuary the Spanish/Mam-speaking congregation and students were framed as "Others" through the institutional power of the religious organization and the legally binding lease that used linguistic differences against them. The English-only or English official movement that pushes for legislation to instantiate English as the official language at the state level demonstrates a proud belief in monolingualism, so long as the single language spoken is English. With thirty-six of the fifty states and US territories legislated with English as the official language (Crawford), English-only legislation demonstrates a dominant belief about the colonizing force of English on Indigenous lands in the US. Liggett draws on CRT as she calls attention to the connection between "English only" and the enduring legacy of colonialism when she writes:

> Contemporary manifestations of colonialism play out in both racial and linguistic discrimination through symbols, expressions, and representations. Today, racial issues stay hidden in terminology such as "colorblind" and "post-racial," while demands for "English Only" have become more vocal and aligned with notions of patriotism, nationalism, and the content of one's character. (116)

For educators this policy severely limits the resources allocated for supporting multilingual literacy practices. As I have previously stated, "English Official demonstrates an enduring colonial project that privileges nativism and excludes non-white multilinguals from institutional power due to linguistic differences that mark multilinguals as 'other'" ("Decolonial Potential" 85). Linguistically marking the Spanish-speaking congregation as Other delegitimizes their rights to discuss the property agreement because the language difference is used to ignore their claims.

However, language should continue being examined, in addition to decolonial frameworks, through a racial lens like CRT because of how discrimination based on race is normalized through the authorization of particular languages and languaging. April Baker Bell explains that "theorizing language through the lens of race provides insightful historical and political analyses of how linguistic racism has been institutionalized" (16). Bilingual education researchers have called for critical race theory scholars to pay attention to English education for Latinx populations because racism impacts Latinx students in more nuanced ways beyond the more obvious policies like "English only." Chávez-Moreno reminds bilingual educators that racism is localized: "It is unsurprising that white supremacy affects language restrictive contexts and bilingual educational settings, such as racially diverse dual-language and even all-Latinx programs" (113). Because the Sanctuary's English program is an all-Latinx program, it might come less as a surprise for CRT scholars that this community of color would face discrimination, like the struggle over the lease, because the allotment of resources such as tax funding for schools operates along racial hierarchies supported by redlining and other environmental racism. Because the signing of a lease can be dismissed as a potential clerical or bureaucratic oversight, this purposeful omission on the part of the English-speaking church serves as an example of the less overt and more everyday instances of discrimination at the intersection of race and language difference.

My participatory role as a volunteer English teacher in the East Bay of Northern California informs my understanding that migrants from outside the US, specifically Central Americans, want and try to "learn the language," even when the language might be their second colonial language. Through interviews and data collected at the Sanctuary through anonymous surveys, I set out to examine the extent to which these migrant populations perceived the goal of learning English as having an impact on their ability to negotiate everyday circumstances and long-term aspirations embodied by the trope of the American Dream, or what Steven Alvarez calls *superarse* (improving one's life). These questions are particularly salient at this moment of entrenched ideological belief in political parties with presidential campaigns that have promised to "make America great again." This belief alludes to the rhetorical power of the trope of the American Dream that upholds the bootstrap myth of hard work that erases the ecologies of power dynamics that impact an individual's ability to succeed (Villanueva). The centrality of how these Indigenous Maya were removed from their lands and left with few options except to learn another dominant language also highlights important issues decolonial theory, practices, and methods address. In the next section, decolonial methods and CRT will be discussed in relation to the collection of data at the Sanctuary in the form of interviews and surveys.

METHOD

In addition to the ethnographic narrative compiled through various notes, interviews, email and letter exchanges, and participant observation, this chapter also draws on responses arrived at through anonymous surveys with undocumented adult students from Guatemala, Honduras, El Salvador, and Mexico. The narrative regarding the Sanctuary's struggle with its lease and the central role of language highlights the material impact on communities of color and the intersectional oppressions that critical race theory articulates. CRT addresses intersecting issues of race, class, citizenship status, and education and acknowledges the prevalence of racism in all aspects of US institutions and society. Aja Martinez reminds us that CRT began with its roots "operating concurrently within multiple forms of social oppression" (*Counterstory* 10) in legal theory, where Derrick Bell ("Serving" and "Brown . . . Interest-Convergence") questioned the objectivity of the legal system in areas such as school desegregation. Bell's discussion of school segregation helps thinking about the Sanctuary because he connects the legal protection of property with school districts impacting property values and property tax generated for school districts. School segregation became an issue for homeowners who believed their property afforded them the right to remain separate. Referring to the landscape of 2000, Bell explains, "many whites resist any change in the 'separate but equal' standard they view as a vested property right. Resistance under these circumstances is no less a manifestation of white victimization because it is willingly accepted and forthrightly maintained" ("Brown . . . Forty-Five Years" 178). At the Sanctuary the unwillingness of the English-speaking congregation to work with the Spanish-speaking congregation can be interpreted as the unwillingness of the predominantly white congregation to feel victimized by having to own up for their transgressions with the lease. This white victimization similarly supports Western expansion and undergirds the narrative of the spirited pioneer who had no other option than to settle stolen Native American land, the very same victimization acted out and normalized through the majority of the cowboy Western film genre.

Relevant to the Sanctuary's struggle over the property's lease, sociologist Mary Romero points out how "CRT immigration researchers recognize that various forms of citizenship status stem from the delineation of rights, privileges, and penalties relative to property, taxes, welfare, and the freedom of movement across nation states" (27). The struggle for the Sanctuary's property interconnects with assumptions about citizenship based on physical appearance and English-speaking ability, which the second tenet of CRT and decolonial theory recognize as grounded in enduring legacies of racism and colonialism.

The recent history of Indigenous Guatemalans can be understood to some extent using decolonial approaches to help untangle the impacts on these communities of people who seek refuge in the US. Cana Uluak Itchuaqiyaq and Breeanne Matheson articulate an actionable definition for decolonial methodologies that aligns with the experiences that no doubt impact the student population at the Sanctuary. They explain that "decolonial methodologies support, respect, and restore the sovereignty of Indigenous peoples, lands, and knowledges. They also support community-developed aspirations for Indigenous peoples, and support the abatement of unjust conditions related to settler colonialism that affect Indigenous communities" (25). The Indigenous Mayan language of Mam spoken by many of the adult Guatemalan students at the Sanctuary and the forced displacement currently practiced in Guatemala highlight the necessity of decolonial approaches to interpreting the enduring impact of colonialism. While the work of the English program at the Sanctuary may be complicit in perpetuating the colonial goals of assimilation, my own pedagogical motivations were grounded in supporting the goals of the migrant students. The work of the English program by the staff of the Sanctuary also extended to community work that went beyond the religious services and covered everything from help with enrolling children in school, to finding access to food, to securing housing.

The location of the East Bay is a locus for issues related to immigration, such as the forces of linguistic and environmental racism facing the migrants looking to *superarse* and who are forced to respond to transnational issues of displacement connected to ongoing neocolonial projects. Drawing on both CRT and decolonial methods in a grounded theory serves the purpose of interpreting contemporary racism and the transnational and historical legacies of coloniality around the social realities facing those at the Sanctuary. Ali Meghji advocates for what he calls a synergy of these methods because they address different temporal moments: "This divergence between decolonial thought's focus on coloniality, and CRT's focus on contemporary racism, creates a methodological difference between historical analysis and presentism" (4). Following Meghji's logic, CRT helps interpret how race impacts issues of citizenship, language, and property, while decolonial theory helps when analyzing transnational factors like land displacement and violence in Guatemala that contributed to migration to the US. This synergy blurs the US/global binary by acknowledging how decolonial methods addressing ongoing neocolonial projects like gentrification impact the present: "Decolonial thought is able to show how the epistemic and material power relations that were born in colonialism continue to shape the present" (Meghji 13). The shaping of the present is particularly relevant when considering factors influencing migration. These factors include the spread of capitalism across Latin America in the form of narco-trafficking incorporating violence as a cost of doing business as well as the colonizing role of gentrification in the East Bay.

In part because of the precarious and vulnerable position of the students' immigration status, I incorporated the anonymous surveys as a method for addressing the widespread commonalities among the students without interviewing each student independently. One of the most important considerations I kept in mind as a participant observer was abiding by the community-building purpose of the church and the English language program. I asked students to fill out surveys and sign informed consent forms in Spanish, with Mateo reiterating and answering questions some students had. I collected data at two separate times during the course of the three years I volunteered, choosing break times during class sessions that were near the end of the terms, when I believed I had earned the trust of the students from them having seen me either over the term or over the multiple terms when we were both there.

On top of the survey data I collected, I also had access to additional surveys taken by Mateo and his spouse Martha for assessment of the ESL program as well as for the additional kinds of church-related activities the students were interested in. This preexisting data had more questions related to religious affiliation and practices, but it also made similar inquiries into reasons for coming to the US, country of origin, and goals. Mateo explained to me that these surveys were meant to help him understand the "felt need" of the community he was serving as a missionary, rather than Mateo telling the community what they needed. Mateo told me that the concept of "felt need" came from a book called *Beyond Charity: The Call to Christian Community Development* by missionary John Perkins. Perkins explains the notion of "felt need" as demonstrated by the story of Jesus's interaction with the Samaritan woman at the well in the book of John, chapter 4. Jesus asks the Samaritan woman for a drink of water rather than telling the woman that if she believes in him, she will never thirst (33). The message follows a somewhat patriarchal logic that the woman does not know what she wants until Jesus tells her. Perkins explains, "Jesus has identified her felt need, and now he will show her that she has a deeper need" (34). Mateo explained, "The concept of felt need supported working in the area without falling into the missionary tradition of planting flags and telling the people what was best for them." Mateo's interpretation of Perkins's approach seems to overlook that the goal is to tell people that Christianity is what is best for them, while acknowledging that they might have other, more immediate needs that a missionary can first address. Decolonial work asks that we pay attention to the colonial role of missionary work as a force that perpetuates beliefs like assimilation. However, some of the more overt violence happening in the migrants' home countries and their religious ambivalence based on the role of religion in their "civil wars" help highlight the positive work of Mateo and the Sanctuary church for these predominantly Indigenous communities. As someone who has known Mateo for many years, I can attest to his earnest desire to be of service for the purpose of sharing with others what brings him joy.

The following sections include findings from the survey data that provoke important aspects of the migrant experience of the adult students at the Sanctuary. Some of the survey responses complicate the linguicism of monolingual ideology and immigration opponents who argue that immigrant populations do not assimilate to the social construct of whiteness and false assumptions about multilingual practices.

MAM MULTILINGUALISM

As noted in previous chapters, Guatemala was by far the most frequently named country of origin for the surveyed adult migrant students, with 85 percent of the survey respondents reporting it as their country of origin. This survey response correlates with a report from the International Organization for Migration, with the number of migrants deported from the US to Guatemala having increased 600 percent between 2004 and 2012 (Taft-Morales 25). This 600 percent increase in deported migrants signals a significant increase in overall migration from Guatemala, although those engaging the heavily politicized topic of immigration rarely delve into ways of addressing the poverty, violence, and failure of governmental institutions that provoke so many to leave. In the US little culpability is offered for the demand of the drug trade that has spread corruption through countries like Guatemala. A journalist interviewed a Honduran intelligence agent who "defended the theory that Guatemala is the center of US-bound cocaine trafficking, full of men trusted by both the Mexicans and Colombians" (O. Martínez, *History* 33). Describing the northern Guatemalan state of Petén, Martínez explains that in the drug trade to the US, "Petén could be called the Central American Golden Gate to Mexico" (62). The 600 percent increase in deported immigrants from Guatemala could very well be accounted for by the displacement of Indigenous campesinos forced from farmland because this land fell along the drug trade route primarily servicing the US consumption of illegal drugs.

Of those surveyed at the Sanctuary, 33 percent had only been in the US for one to two years. The self-described level of English by those in the US one to two years ranged from "no English" to "a little bit" in responses. These responses are particularly salient not only because the length of time in the US paralleled the time the classes were offered but, more importantly, because they show the students' desire to learn English and their willingness to participate in programs when they became available. Even in the nontraditional education space of a church basement, I often found myself in the teacher mindset of keeping a particular pace during the class session to account for the class size of twenty to thirty. I moved around the room, hoping to speak slowly and clearly enough while making eye contact, often disconnected from the realities of these men and women who had recently arrived. The pride I might have experienced as a volunteer teacher on nights when a class session went well was naive, very much like the average US citizen who seems confused about migrants circumventing the bewildering immigration system when neither the teacher nor the average US citizen can recognize the fear, the pain, and the sacrifice that went into that class participation and decision.

The attempts of so many of the students to learn English in their first year of arriving to the US, in spite of the language being used against them by the English-speaking congregation, further underscore the racial component motivating this discrimination. Baker-Bell reminds us to consider how these issues remain interrelated: "Linguistic hierarchies and racial hierarchies are interconnected. That is, people's language experiences are not separate from their racial experiences" (2). Arguments for migrants to "learn the language"

98 • CHAPTER 4

should be recognized as little more than arguments for learning enough English to become more efficient disposable labor without rights or a promise of citizenship. When the linguistic abilities of the students and congregation were used as reasons for the two congregations not getting along, this was little more than English speakers attempting to exert what power they felt entitled to as a part of the racial and linguistic hierarchy.

In a conversation I had with a student named Ramón, he said, "I like practicing English." He was also quite fluent in comparison to many of the beginners. He said, "At work, a lot of my coworkers only speak Spanish. And then at home, I only speak Spanish." Ramón's experience serves as a reminder that for migrants, there aren't always many opportunities to practice English, even when living in the US. As noted previously, CRT scholar Derrick Bell describes the "separate but equal" policy in education as something many white Americans "willingly accepted and forthrightly maintained" ("Brown . . . Forty-Five Years" 178); this entrenched segregation begins in hospitals and schools and continues through housing and workplace discrimination. As someone working at a private institution of higher education, I do not interact with many young people like Ramón by design, as private campuses monitor and intercept people racially profiled on campus by private security and local police (Elassar; Ore).

In a conversation with one of my students, Pedro, who looks to be in his late twenties or early thirties, the topic of multilingualism and its impact on families and communities surfaced. Pedro had long hair to his shoulders and was slightly taller than some of the other students, with an athletic build. Pedro drove forklifts in a warehouse and seemed more comfortable speaking than some of the other students in the class, perhaps because he could have passed for someone who had grown up in the US. However, he told me that what still gave him problems was writing in English. Pedro said, "It is different than how we speak [English]." For those of us who teach writing, we are often confronted with the gatekeeping role that being able to perform "standard academic English" can play, often to the exclusion of our working-class students and students of color who do not have access to the preparation required for being dubbed "a good writer." Pedro no doubt saw the limitations of learning English in terms of what access would be afforded to him and how writing added an additional layer of marginalization.

According to the surveys I circulated, two-thirds (66 percent) of the students were in their first year of learning English. This number on its own highlights the lack of infrastructure available to people who will be subsumed by the market economy and put to work for their physical labor. What the statistic of 66 percent of students being in their first year of learning English still does not reveal is the varying levels of literacy in the classes, with some older students having never attended school. For Pedro, learning to write in English serves as an additional barrier, while for many of these students without previous school experience, their possibility of moving beyond conversational English can be extremely difficult. In the US we continue to see arguments for English-only education that appeal to an ideology "aligned with notions of patriotism, nationalism, and the content of one's character" (Liggett 116); yet, they overlook how many migrants try to learn English with very few public resources to facilitate this learning. Such is certainly the case with Pedro and the other students at the Sanctuary.

Advocates of English-only laws argue for linguistic policy based on a monolingual ideology that forwards a nationalist rhetoric that vilifies migrants and portrays them as inferior. English-only ideology discriminates by positioning home languages as deficient in comparison to English, which is held up as power for whites. Steven Alvarez explains that "subtractive English-only ideologies dynamically positioned communities' home practices as deficient, as schools policed language discrimination. These ideologies are also inherent in language policies which, in turn, are internalized by students as assessable abilities or deficiencies" ("Rhetorical" 89). Ideologies that support English-only policies highlight the intersections that both critical race theory and decolonial theory address because of how versions of Standard English are conflated with whiteness and how English has spread through colonialism and the purposeful erasure of Indigenous languages.

Pedro and I talked about speaking Spanish with our sons at home. He said his seven-year-old son speaks Spanish better than English. I said, "It must be difficult for the people here who speak another language." Pedro said, "I also speak Mam." According to the eighteenth edition of *Ethnologue: Languages of the World,* 530,000 people speak the Mayan language of Mam in Guatemala (Lewis et al.), which is 30.8 percent of the 16.34 million population reported in 2015 (World Bank). The percentage of Mam speakers in Guatemala is remarkably similar to the percentage of Mam speakers at the Sanctuary. At the Sanctuary 30 percent of men and 40 percent of women report speaking Mam as their first language. Teaching English at the Sanctuary, I considered my ability to speak Spanish and explain some of the workbook exercises in Spanish to students as something that made me an especially qualified volunteer; however, during those first several months, I fell victim to assuming I knew the linguistic backgrounds of all students. Linguist and writing scholar Paul Kei Matsuda points out that many writing teachers unwittingly fall victim to assuming the homogeneity of their classroom in terms of linguistic backgrounds and abilities and teaching to assumed student identity.

Pedro said, "My son doesn't like to learn Mam, even though me and my wife speak it." The loss of language in bilingual migrant families is a common occurrence (Portes and Hao), so learning a third language would prove even more difficult. For Latinxs in the US, the loss of Spanish within families can impact both core values and cultural identity: "With language shift, the language loss that may follow represents a loss of 'more crucial core values' and a part of one's identity that is associated with cultural and ethnic groups (Lanza and Svendsen)" (Alvarez, "Rhetorical" 90). Juan Guerra also noted how some of the tensions between Mexican migrants and Chicanx locals in Chicago resulted from Mexican migrants being "disturbed by the inability or unwillingness of many Chicanos to speak Spanish, something that immigrants know marks them as recently arrived Mexicanos" (8). The ability to speak a heritage language can be complicated by tensions to adopt the language of a new space where fitting in with the dominant group surpasses familial and cultural pressures within a community.

I asked Pedro, "Do you speak Mam with many of the other students?"

"No," he said. "I never know who speaks it."

As a Latino in the US, I sympathize with Pedro's situation with Mam because many US Latinxs have the same experience with Spanish. In both instances, different colonial influences disrupted and "created a division within communities when some Indigenous peoples urbanized, spoke the colonizers' languages, or . . . adopted colonizers' religions," resulting in the "fragmentation and artificial hierarchies that generated discord and a crumbling of Indigenous political organization" (Wane 163). Gloria Anzaldúa captures this experience when she plainly states, "Repeated attacks on our native tongue diminish our sense of self" (80). Like Spanish, many dialects of Mam further complicate the level to which people from the same country can communicate in their native languages. In addition, the thirty-six years of the "civil war" / *la violencia* in Guatemala left a long-lasting sense of distrust because of the use of Native informants by the Guatemalan military, which disrupted the social fabric of Maya communities that can still be felt to this day (Green; Ujpán; Zur).

During a break between classes, Dori, a new teacher, joined a table in the church's basement where students were drinking coffee and eating sections of pan dulce the Sanctuary staff cut into smaller pieces and set out for students. Dori used to volunteer and teach English at the Sanctuary when the program was organized by a previous group before Mateo. Like Mateo, Dori had learned Spanish in Costa Rica, although she also has family in El Salvador. As we drank the warm, weak coffee, I mentioned to Dori how many of the students spoke Mam, in relation to whatever topic about teaching English we were discussing. Dori asked the students sitting at the long line of bench tables next to us, "Do you all speak Mam?"

They nodded, saying they indeed spoke Mam. Dori looked surprised, caught off guard by this new information. Two of the advanced students, Rolando and Juan, smiled and said, "Everyone speaks Mam."

Dori asked, "Do you speak Mam with each other?"

They said they did not, citing the fact that everyone tends to speak different dialects.

"I couldn't understand him and he couldn't understand me if we speak Mam," Rolando said. According to *A Grammar of Mam, a Mayan Language* by Nora England, there is limited contact between Mam-speaking communities, so the language can vary between communities. Further, the Guatemalan Academy of Mayan Languages shows that Mam is spoken in 64 communities across four Guatemalan provinces (Quetzaltenango, Huehuetenango, San Marcos, and Retalhuleu). For this reason, even though "everyone speaks Mam," the students communicate among themselves primarily in the colonial language of Spanish. However, the explanation of "limited contact between Mam communities" belies the darker reasons stemming from Guatemala's history of "civil war" / *la violencia* that continues to maintain the divides between Indigenous languages. There has been a great deal of mistrust among Guatemalans following the "civil war" / *la violencia*. In Guatemala, Indigenous Maya have discriminated against other groups of Maya: "Indians meekly refer to themselves as 'little natural people' (*naturalcitos*) but barely hesitate to describe Indians from other ethnic groups . . . as less civilized and less worthy, 'not too bright' or 'idiots'" (Zur 34). Whether these negative characterizations are rooted in long-held beliefs or whether the division among the Indigenous Maya comes as a colonial strategy of conquest, *la violencia* contributed to further entrenching these divisions with mistrust. This mistrust stemmed from allegations of being associated with guerillas leading to disappearance and death by the counterinsurgency military. Fear and mistrust were a part of the terror the government inflicted because there was often "no satisfactory explanation for the deaths" of husbands and sons disappeared by the military populated by Maya who aligned themselves with the Ladino government (Zur 11).

THE SANCTUARY'S STRUGGLE

Following the meeting where the lease was supposed to be discussed by the denomination's leadership, the leadership of the Sanctuary continued strategizing about how to approach the issue. On a few occasions when I arrived at the Sanctuary to teach, meetings with members of the congregation were taking place in the classroom where I taught.

On one of these days, members sat quietly around the large rectangular desk in the center of the small room. Isabel asked me, "Do you need copies from the workbook?" The expressions of the attendees at the meetings were tense, their brows furrowed and voices sharp with concern. "The meeting will soon be over," Isabel said. As my students began to show up, the group moved their meeting into the front pews of the church.

For the migrant population at the Sanctuary, like for many migrants in the US, learning English was viewed as a step toward gaining access to citizenship. Because the English language classes at the Sanctuary relied on volunteer teachers and the space provided by the church, the educational inequality was readily visible. The humble resources and emotional labor diverted from this student population reveal the impact of privileging property over people. In "Toward a Critical Race Theory of Education," Gloria Ladson-Billings and William F. Tate explain that "the intersection of race and property creates an analytic tool through which we can understand social (and, consequently, school) inequality" (48). Additionally, the intersection of race and property as an analytic tool highlights the struggle between the congregations because of the neocolonial desire for land.

On one Monday evening during the prayer Isabel led prior to the beginning of classes, she asked, "Would anyone like to ask for anything special to be mentioned during prayers?" No one spoke up. She led the prayer and afterward announced the Thanksgiving dinner that the church would be hosting for everyone who would like to come. She said, "It's for you, the students here, and anyone you would like to bring. And it's for the members of the church." She added, "We want you all to think of the church as a refuge, as more than class, as a community where you can come to feel safe." She continued, "Many of us are aware of what's happening with the church's struggles."

A student raised his hand and said he was unaware, so Isabel explained that for the last few years, the other church had tried to get the Sanctuary congregation out of the church. Isabel added, "The prayers and efforts of the students will be what keep us here."

Isabel's strong connection with the Sanctuary and the future of the property follows what American Indian rhetorical scholars have argued about the centrality of land to not just Indigenous populations, but also for the teaching of Indigenous rhetorics. Isabel's connection to the Sanctuary involved more than just the building; it was to the spirit of the place, embodied by Indigenous scholars who argue that "this understanding of how we are connected to the land, how we are an extension of the land . . . is critical to understanding how we teach indigenous rhetorics" (Rain Anderson 161). Indigenous rhetorics are central to the decolonial practice of untangling the enduring projects of colonialism that attempt to displace and erase Native populations in the changing name of modernity. Discussions of land and citizenship are fraught within colonial matrices that dehumanize people subjected to these ecologies that root out deeper connections to land and communal space.

During the prayer that precedes class on another Monday evening, Isabel asked if there was anyone who would like the group to pray for them. The normal moment of awkward silence was broken by an older woman I recognized who stood up and asked, "Could you pray for help with my depression?" She began to cry, adding, "It has been hard."

With this woman's request, the very mundane space of the church basement made the uncertainty, insecurity, and loneliness of the migrant experience fill the room with an enormity of helplessness. Psychologists who studied the depression rate in Latina migrant mothers who were separated from their children found that the odds of depression were 1.52 times greater for those Latina mothers whose children were not living with them (Miranda et al.). Politicians point to the millions of dollars, or 23 percent of unpaid hospital bills, attributed to undocumented migrants (Urrea 180), but the people seeking medical care only tend to do so because they fear for their lives or the lives of their children from prolonged illness or life-threatening injury. Meanwhile, these populations suffer in silence as they carry with them the traumas occurring in their home countries, their fear for family back at home, and the feelings of hopelessness that sink in if they cannot find work.

When Isabel said I could interview her, she was busy as usual, so I followed her around the Sanctuary before classes as she greeted and helped those exiting and entering the building. I asked her some questions about the English program. In a short moment between fielding requests and questions from students entering the building, she described how she saw the many roles of the Sanctuary: "I believe that here, it's not a secular school. It's more of a refuge, a home where they can have freedom and attend to their spiritual needs. If they have needs like food, groceries—I think that's one of the attributes of the program that the people collaborate to have this empathy, this sensibility for the students, for the language." Isabel was the person at the Sanctuary who could get things done, although she too undoubtedly had to recognize her limits. In some cases, the only aid that could be offered was a supportive prayer. Isabel's work contributes to the tradition of literacy work within churches Beverly Moss describes as "a complex, social process involving multiple levels of participation by rhetors and audience, intertextual relationships (i.e., interdependent relations between oral, written, and sometimes musical texts) and complex belief systems of members of particular communities" (6). Though the English program's curriculum of the Sanctuary did not include

104 • CHAPTER 4

explicit material about the church's belief system, the ecology of the space and the beliefs of many of the volunteer teachers aligned, often intertwining pedagogical exigency with the language-acquisition practices in the classrooms.

A couple weeks later, I met Mateo for lunch. I parked near the house where he and his spouse Martha lived with their infant son in a second-story bungalow at the back of a small single-family home. His landlord, an older woman from Guatemala, said she could not come to the English classes anymore when he introduced me as a teacher at the Sanctuary. We ate Mexican food around the corner from his house and walked his son around the block, all the while talking about the future of the Sanctuary. As we walked, Mateo stopped to speak to a few different people, mostly women, some with children, and most of them introduced him to others around them through his work as a teacher at the church. We passed a line formed around a corner for free food, mostly women with roller carts to carry home bags of potatoes, chips, and such. Mateo said, "I'm thinking about the future, after my time here [in the East Bay]."

When I talked to Mateo about the fate of the church, he was hesitant to make any definitive declarations based on his observations of the meetings between the two congregations he had been asked to attend. He said he attended talks for the church, acting as an intermediary language broker. He said there was a long history between the two congregations. He noted, "There was a woman from the English-speaking church who spoke in a very accusatory way, raising concerns about the upkeep of the [Sanctuary's church] building."

Mateo explained that he thought the concern about the building seemed to overlook the good work done at the church and did not help with the churches coming to any reconciliation. Unlike Isabel, Pastor Pablo, and the Spanish-speaking congregation, Mateo was much more philosophical about the situation. He said that he thought the Sanctuary's Spanish service and English-language classes didn't need to stay at that location. Mateo's definition of what the Sanctuary provides was not limited by the physical walls of the Sanctuary building.

"It's just a building," he said. "I believe people could meet in someone's house if need be." But he also conceded the benefit of a centralized location where people knew they could come to meet. Mateo's vocation as a missionary in itself is more transitory than the more entrenched space of the Sanctuary and less concerned with the decolonial goal "to create, sustain, and maintain a habitable space for present and future generations" (Mukavetz 126). Perhaps because Mateo's primary goal as a missionary supersedes his role in the English program, he could be more philosophical about where his work could happen. Because the adult migrant students no doubt experience the power

STRUGGLE, DISCRIMINATION, AND DISPLACEMENT • 105

discrepancy between themselves and the English program staff, they might feel hesitant about pushing back against spiritual goals in favor of their goal of literacy acquisition at the Sanctuary.

CONCLUSION

Some of the nuances of the Sanctuary's relationship with the English-speaking church came into focus through conversations with Nielly, a volunteer English teacher, who served in a pastoral role of the same denomination as the Sanctuary at a different location. Nielly was a friendly woman in her early thirties with glasses and curly, dark blond hair. She often brought her guitar and sang songs with her classes as a part of her class sessions. I asked her what she knew about the situation with the church next door. She scrunched up her face and explained, "My church doesn't really interact with the other [English-speaking] church. I'm not sure if very many people go to that church." She added, "It always seems empty when I'm here to teach."

This chapter and the story of the struggle with the lease both end somewhat in a place of uncertainty. At the end of my three years at the Sanctuary, the situation was not rectified. The Sanctuary staff and congregation continued to worry they were going to be evicted. Uncertainty about the Sanctuary's future hung heavy in the air until the stress became normalized. It was almost as through the precarious state of undocumented migrants was manifested into the walls of the Sanctuary building, which felt like it could be taken away at any moment.

A year or so later, when Mateo had completed his sabbatical, I had a chance to meet up with him. He told me that at some point after I stopped teaching, the English-speaking congregation left. "No one really saw them go," Mateo said. "They just seemed to disappear without telling anyone."

The staff and congregation at the Sanctuary are still there, continuing with English classes and other community-oriented services. It was unclear from what Mateo said whether the English-speaking church stayed for the duration of the lease or simply quit it. What mattered was that the Spanish-speaking Sanctuary congregation was allowed to stay.

The Sanctuary's lease situation unfortunately demonstrates the material realities of how standard English can be used as distortion against migrant communities to silence and exclude. By circumventing communication between the two churches, the English-speaking congregation failed to accommodate and embodied "the practice of invoking standards not to improve communication and assist language learners, but to exclude voices and perspectives at odds with those in power" (Horner et al. 305). It is a tragic irony that at a site of voluntary teaching and learning of English, the success and future of the church and its classes would be threatened by those using linguistic difference and linguicism as a form of control over property meant as a refuge. The relationship between the Sanctuary and its neighboring English congregation might only seem to reflect the microcosm of the communities impacted by the power imbalance supported by monolingual ideology. However, the divide between the churches speaks to the national political divide that is further entrenched by public appeals to white supremacist ideology on the part of political leaders.

At the same time, treating migrants as rhetorical scapegoats is a topos of politics that is carried out in the laws that reaffirm inclusion and exclusion. An *Emory Law Journal* article underscores how the rejection of asylum seekers was business as usual even under the Biden administration:

> The Biden DHS [Department of Homeland Security] has maintained the status quo and prevented migrants from accessing asylum—a right enshrined under domestic and international law—and detained asylum seekers en masse in an ever-expanding network of ICE [Immigration and Customs Enforcement] prisons. (Shahshahani and Gosrani 1264)

In spite of domestic and international law, the immigration system continues to show how it was designed for the exclusion of nonwhite immigrants through the selective adherence to laws when it suits the system.

In the next chapter, counterstory provides a methodology for responding to the dominant narratives about Indigenous literacy beliefs and practices from the perspectives of those with lived experiences that differ from the stock stories on these topics. One dominant narrative about migrants that appears in this chapter and the next is that migrants do not "learn the language." The church has been offering classes for just over three years, and many of the advanced English-speaking students explain that finding opportunities to speak English can be difficult, especially because many of them work with other Spanish speakers. The multilingual linguistic practices of immigrants from Guatemala suggest a worldview about language that is more receptive to language acquisition than the monolingual ideology of those singularly privileging the acquisition of English.

At the same time, our own limitations as educators come up against the strains from lacking resources, dwindling attendance, and not seeing students succeed beyond our classrooms. These limitations are outside of our control and are often designed as part of the inequalities within our systems that we negotiate and attempt to come to terms with, ideally before it breaks us.

CHAPTER 5

Volunteer Literacy
Teacher Counterstory

LITERACY EXPECTATIONS OF WHITE SUPREMACY

On the night the student named Carlos was assaulted outside the Sanctuary, the class began with the excited energy that comes with the end of a school term. It was the second-to-last week of the spring session in 2015, and I was pleasantly surprised by the consistent attendance of students who had come the last ten weeks or so. I felt energized by the progress of the class, the closeness I felt to them, and the wistful nostalgia of knowing a term is coming to an end.

Arriving early, I lifted and moved the bench tables that had been put up in the corner of the basement. There had been a wedding in the church, with the reception in the basement the night before. Isabel was running late with some business upstairs, so I asked Juan, one of the older students in my class, to lead the Monday night prayer so that we might begin the classes; Juan had led the prayer in the past with Isabel, and he dutifully accepted.

Just before the break, Isabel entered my classroom and made an announcement. She said, "I want to remind everyone that if you sign up and pay now, you will be guaranteed a spot in the next session. This is important because the program will be limiting the class sizes for the students who are committed."

To encourage buy-in from the students to complete the class sessions that went for about the duration of my university's ten-week quarter, Isabel suggested having the students pay a nominal price of twenty dollars or so to register for the classes. The rationale was that students were more likely to commit to something that they paid for, with the money going toward workbooks and modest gift cards for the volunteer teachers at the end of the sessions. Isabel said that the gift cards for the teachers served as a gesture of thanks, which students had told her that they wanted to do in some way to show their appreciation.

During the break, I spoke with a couple of the older women in my group. Rosa, an older woman from Mexico with adult children, asked me, "Are you always in a good mood?"

When teaching, I find that my classroom persona ranges on a spectrum depending on the energy of the students. Because the class was full of adults who have worked manual labor jobs and chose to come to two hours of classes and followed classroom instructions without hesitation or resistance, I wanted to bring as much of my own energy as possible to the class. Some days I would stop at the Spanish-speaking market down the street from the Sanctuary to pick up a large energy drink for added pep. In English and Spanish, I tried to make jokes to the class when appropriate to model the playfulness to experiment that can help when learning a new language.

When we returned from the break, a lot of students lingered in the breezeway of the Sanctuary, outside the classroom door. Not all the students were back in the classroom, but those who were spoke in hushed tones to each other.

I asked, "What happened? Where is everyone?"

Rosa said, "A student was attacked on the street outside the church."

When more of the students trickled in, we found out that the student who was attacked was a good-natured man named Carlos. He was attacked on the street corner, a hundred yards or so from the church's entrance. During the break, he had gone home. It was only a couple minutes away down the busy street that led toward the freeway. As he waited for the light at the crosswalk to change on his way back, a car pulled up, and two African American men jumped out and ran toward him. One put a gun to Carlos's head and told Carlos to give him his money. The man took his money and cell phone. He then punched Carlos in the stomach before he and the other man hopped back in their car and sped off. Carlos ran back to the church, where someone called the police. Shaken up and a bit sore where he'd been hit, he said, "I'm okay." To explain why he had gone home during the break, he said, "To get money to sign up for the next classes."

Unlike traditional educational institutions with state and local funding, the Sanctuary relied on volunteer labor from their English teachers. One of the factors my fellow volunteer teachers reported influencing their returning to teach had to do with the time and effort it took to volunteer in the evenings after a full day of work and family obligations. Several times new teachers would be really excited to start, but they would burn out after volunteering to teach multiple nights a week. The time commitment was too much, and they would stop coming altogether. The inconsistent attendance of students in classes as weeks went on could eat away at any sense of altruism. The Sanctuary's desire to generate buy-in from the students put Carlos into the dangerous position of trying to get money by himself during the break. Due to the legal status of many of the students at the Sanctuary, the staff and Mateo were leery and uncertain about securing funding that might benefit the program; as it was, the Sanctuary staff made do with what little money the church had to address more life-threatening issues like food insecurity and the housing of its members and those seeking assistance. Unfortunately, Carlos's experience is something of a metonymy for many migrants who sacrifice to better themselves and, in doing so, are put into a dangerous position where they are subject to being preyed upon with little recourse because they have already been criminalized.

The violence committed against migrants like Carlos is perpetuated by the dominant narratives like those expressed by Donald Trump about Mexico and other countries "not sending their best" (Neate) and characterizing migrants as criminals and disposable labor. Because migrant populations like the adult students at the Sanctuary are portrayed as criminals by the dominant narrative espoused by President Trump and others in power, these populations are thought of as deficient, even though their lived experiences complicate and resist what critical race theory scholars call "majoritarian" tales (Delgado and Stefancic; A. Martinez, *Counterstory*; Yosso). Majoritarian stories are told from a place of racial privilege and often fall into the "stock" stories that rely on the essentialist logic of stereotypes. Trump's rhetoric of other countries "not sending their best" misrepresents how many who migrate do so because of the danger or lack of options they face at home. Often when migrants risk their lives to arrive in the US, they perform manual labor, like many of the men at the Sanctuary who work construction or clean buildings and homes. These kinds of jobs play into elitist stock stories that these less-skilled positions are indicative of less intelligence or less desire and ability to learn.

This chapter follows the methodology of counterstory from critical race theory that speaks back to the dominant narratives about the Indigenous Maya campesinos from Guatemala. This counterstory responds to those stock stories misrepresenting migrants as criminals who do not want to learn by acknowledging some of the barriers they face, including policies that impact their access to education. Even though this migrant population of adult students at the Sanctuary wants to learn and even provides feedback for improving their education, they still lack either access or the resources to access institutional learning spaces. Though I do not belong to this group and it is not my testimony to give, this counterstory comes from the perspective of someone who spent three years teaching this Indigenous migrant population and is informed by traditional academic scholarship that provides statistical data and findings for additional context. Through my experiences with these students, I present a counternarrative that speaks back to educational criticism raised by another volunteer teacher that is indicative of the dominant narratives circulated in Guatemala and in the US about literacy and knowledge.

COUNTERSTORY AS METHOD

As a methodology informed by critical race theory, counterstory provides the necessary method for identifying matrices of dominant narratives about migrants, using the perspectives of migrant students at the Sanctuary as well as research on campesino and Indigenous Latin American populations. Rhetoric scholar Aja Martinez explains how CRT methodology functions "as a challenge to 'majoritarian' stories or 'master narratives' of white privilege. This methodology rejects notions of 'neutral' research or 'objective' research and exposes research that silences and distorts epistemologies of people of color" (*Counterstory* 3). As a part of the goal of decolonizing how immigration is discussed through colonial paradigms protecting those in power, counterstory offers a method for pushing back against majoritarian narratives of assimilation within literacy studies that tacitly promise economic success by acquiring literacy.

The methodology of counterstory is relevant to this chapter about the dominant narratives that teachers can perpetuate because the racist education policy that serves to exclude nonwhites intersects with the citizenship status of the students who experience greater challenges to educational access despite majoritarian narratives arguing for immigrants to learn the language. The first tenet of critical race theory in education, "focusing on racisms," highlights intersecting discriminations because of the immigration and language discrimination students face: "A CRT in education centralizes race and racism, while also focusing on racisms' intersections with other forms of subordination, based on gender, class, sexuality, language, culture, immigrant status, phenotype, accent, and surname" (Yosso 7). The subtle racism the students experience at the Sanctuary and the exclusion from traditional educational institutions bring to light issues of language, culture, and immigration status.

Racism's exclusionary impact in subtle and even systemic ways positions the adult students as less intelligent or less capable of making decisions for themselves as a result of majoritarian narratives.

In "Digital Latinx Storytelling: Testimonio as Multimodal Resistance," I draw on Latinx critical race theory, or LatCrit, in research on digital testimonio, advocating for the digital storytelling genre as part of a pedagogy that is culturally relevant and that provides a space to speak truth to power for students of color. I point to the centrality of storytelling in LatCrit that can be leveraged with the affordances of multimedia in digital spaces: "The genre of digital testimonio is undergirded by the centrality of experiential knowledge in LatCrit scholarship that challenges the dominant narratives normalizing and dismissing the systemic oppression of people and communities of color" (Medina, "Digital"). In addition, I coauthored a response with Aja Martinez to academic scholarship that relied on stock stories to flatten the nuances about the lives impacted by anti-Latinx laws in Arizona. In doing so, we explain that "counterstory functions as a method for marginalized people to intervene in research methods that would form master narratives based on ignorance and on assumptions about minoritized peoples like Chican@s" (Medina and Martinez). Richard Delgado, Derrick Bell, and Patricia J. Williams represent "counterstory exemplars" who push back against dominant narratives grounded in white supremacy: "Because white people do not often acknowledge the experiences of people of color, the crits [critical race theorists] recognize and have developed the methodology of counterstory to relate the racial realities of people of color while also providing methods for minoritized people to challenge [majoritarian narratives]" (A. Martinez, *Counterstory* 15). Challenging majoritarian dominant narratives is important because they frame BIPOC communities as deficient compared to whites as these stereotypical stock stories uphold status-quo myths of white supremacy. The use of counterstory in this chapter builds on my past advocacy for testimonio, a method of counterstory, because counterstory provides a necessary method for speaking back as best I can as someone who has lived experiences with a population that is misrepresented in areas such as education, intelligence, criminality, and reasons for immigrating.

In the counterstory that follows, the master narrative about migrants not wanting to further their education is upended with further context of educational obstacles and Indigenous knowledge rooted in land-based practices that speak to pluriversal epistemologies existing. Pluriversal epistemologies include knowledge traditions occurring at what Walter Mignolo calls different loci of enunciation (*Darker*), which are often regarded as colonial and decolonial traditions, yet at the same time recognizing the potential for the knowledges and the worlds that we do not yet know and have not categorized. While I am not an Indigenous Latin American migrant like the students who are the subjects of the racial exclusion, I employ counterstory following the rubric Aja Martinez articulates to qualify for the genre and methodology: "A rubric for counterstory resides in whether the story is informed by the tenets toward advancing a better understanding of how law or policy operate" (*Counterstory* 16). With the passage of bills like Proposition 187 in California, which cut off undocumented people from educational and medical services (Hasian and Delgado), counterstory provides a method for responding to assumptions about Latinx migrants and education. Immigration and foreign policy are often politicized and portrayed from a perspective relying on essentialism, such as the remarks about Mexican immigrants by Donald Trump. Counterstory is therefore necessary for untangling education with language structures linked to an immigration policy that disadvantages nonwhite English-learning migrants. As someone who shares lived experiences in the educational space of the Sanctuary, I offer my counterstory to speak back to prevailing assumptions about Latinx immigrant students.

CLASS SIZE AND MIGRANT STUDENTS
"NOT WANTING TO LEARN MORE"

On the night Carlos was attacked, the students and I could not focus on the workbook material as the police arrived and took Carlos's account in the next room. Instead, the students began to exchange stories about people they knew who experienced violence that seemed to occur without warning. The older woman from Mexico, Rosa, recounted the story of a man she knew who got shot while he was being robbed. She punctuated the story by saying, "And all he had on him was two dollars."

Juan, the student who sometimes led Monday prayer, said, "I was riding my bike down the busy street near the church. It was the middle of the day, and a man with a gun stepped out into the street and stopped me. The man took my money and hit me in the face with the gun. When I went to the hospital with my eye bruised and my mouth busted, they asked if I wanted to report it to the police. But I said I was too scared." Juan's experience exemplifies how anti-immigrant rhetoric serves to make migrants larger targets of violence because of their perceived precarious legal position.

Over the course of the class discussion that evening, we spoke about the words "dangerous" and "danger" in English, and I asked the students if it was dangerous in their own countries. Rosa said "yes," and those from Guatemala said "certain parts," and another said "no." The lack of willingness to discuss violence with any kind of authority figure is something discussed in greater detail in chapter 3, and I did not push for more explanation. The students seem to shy away from speaking in any great detail about violence in their home countries outside of this moment when Carlos was attacked, perhaps out of learned fear of the drug traffickers: A 2014 article reported that "crime and violence have been extremely high in recent years, and officials estimated that up to 60% of Guatemalan territory may be under the effective control of drug traffickers" (Taft-Morales 9–10). I wanted to create a space in the classroom for processing what had happened without pressuring students to discuss anything that might make them feel uncomfortable.

In addition to asking about their feelings about violence in the East Bay, I decided to seek feedback from the students about the class because the somber mood would make carrying on with any kind of formal lesson feel jarring. In education, advocates for decolonial pedagogy center the need for self-determination in the face of following a rigid curriculum. Indigenous education scholar Njoki Nathani Wane argues that self-determination is necessary for decolonial pedagogical projects that "reframe the notion of the internationalization of the curriculum" (161). Sitting around the conference table in our classroom on the ground level, I asked the students what they liked about classes, to which they responded "reading," "writing," and "speaking." When I asked what could improve the classes, they said small class sizes with the same teacher every night and one more class a week, making it four instead of three. Rosa summed it up when she said, "If the same teachers taught all of the classes each week, then they would know what we already covered, and we wouldn't review the same material."

"I agree," I responded. "These are all good ideas." Knowing that a lot of these aspects were interrelated because of the different volunteers teaching the same material at different times, I felt painfully aware that my own inability to teach more frequently made me complicit in slowing the pace of their education. The students followed directions in class by writing down what they were directed to copy from the board or completing a page from the workbook as instructed. As someone who has taught college-level courses for more than a decade, I felt I could be doing a better job of preparing lessons, activities, and class sessions that broke from the regimented exercises of the book or copying from the board. During the first year I was there, I had tried to experiment more with different practices. I printed out different exercises I had found online and made copies to bring to class. Still, the workbook helped with consistency in a program with both inconsistent teachers and students. In addition, our program could have benefited the students with "the involvement of community elders who fill the gaps that textbooks leave" (Wane 170). The interactions with the Sanctuary leadership and staff could have fulfilled this role, although the central focus on the religious purpose of the church could make it difficult to bring additional knowledge traditions.

Because of the traffic-filled commute to the Sanctuary, my institution's teaching load, and my responsibilities at the time as a father of two children under the age of four, I often used the *Step by Step* workbook as the backbone of sessions to create consistency in my lessons and because it was a text many students owned and could return to. When identifying the effective qualities of successful Indigenous education projects, Wane notes that these "models are not 'one size fits all.' They adjust and adapt to local or cultural conditions" (169). Many times I would do activities that were not in the book during the second half of the classes. After the break, it always helped to vary the activities, sometimes with games that included newly learned vocabulary—sometimes acted out in front of the class, sometimes as a group pop quiz of sorts. It lacked the technological infrastructure of most universities, where detailed PowerPoints with multimedia embedded could be projected onto large screens for everyone to see.

When I had printed out additional worksheets I found from ESL resources online, I would do so in the beginning of the term, when there were more students who came with regularity. Education scholar Angela Valenzuela explains how much of language learning programs in schools that actually receive funding follow a "subtractive" curriculum. And while they "are designed to transition youth into an English-only curriculum, they neither reinforce their native language skills nor their cultural identities" (26). In the last weeks of each session, when fewer students tended to show with regularity, the workbook became the main tool when only a few students finished out the session. Losing students over the course of a term can feel disheartening, although Wane reminds us of research in Australia where "many Aboriginal students had to disconnect or disengage from learning in order to survive psychologically" (166–67). Whether it was simply the repetition of textbook lessons or other pedagogically related influences, the dwindling attendance could not be attributed only to the students.

●

When I returned after summer, in the fall of 2015, I had some of the same students even though it was the beginning of a new quarter. When I arrived at the Sanctuary that evening, I spoke with the advanced teacher, Jackie, who had returned from a break, not having volunteered over the summer. Jackie had been teaching at the Sanctuary as long as, if not longer than, I had. For her day job, she taught elementary school and had grown children in their twenties. She appreciated the Sanctuary students because she never had to worry about classroom management with the adult student population. However, she voiced some frustration when she said, "A lot of the students in my class were students I've had in class and taught for the past couple of years, without any new students entering the advanced class from the intermediate levels."

I told Jackie, "Mateo emailed me and the other intermediate teacher asking us if we could let the church know who could possibly move into the advanced level, so maybe you'll get a few new students."

"I went and got the information for a local school where they might be able to take more classes." She exhaled and said, "I just don't want to spend time teaching students who already know what I'm covering."

Some of the advanced students in the class Jackie taught had been in the same class for many sessions, with a few new students joining each time. She said, "I feel like the class would benefit from the students who had been in the class for some time transferring into classes in a community college where they could continue learning beyond what they had seemed to have been continually reviewing in the advanced class."

I was unsure whether Jackie was aware that the community college system in California had exorbitantly higher tuition rates for "out-of-state" students or undocumented people who could not legally demonstrate they had lived in the state for more than a year. Many students lived in places that did not require paperwork, which helped them to secure housing; however, this lack of a paper trail negatively impacted their ability to establish residency. One of the volunteer English teachers at the Sanctuary who came from Honduras told me that after tuition and books, "It costs something like two thousand dollars a semester." This put the kind of formal education Jackie advocated for out of reach for most of the students who struggle with Bay Area rent, cost of living, and labor-intensive jobs. During my class, I talked to some individuals like Mercedes, Gerald, and Rosa, who had been in the class before, about moving up to the next level. They seemed hesitant. During the class, I would jokingly say, "You are so good at English. You should try the advanced class."

At the end of class, one of the Sanctuary's staff named Ana asked if I had any students I thought could go up to the next level. I suggested the few who had been in the class before as well as a new young woman who asked a lot of questions and seemed to understand a majority of the class material with little difficulty. I also recommended Gerald, a student I'd known from

116 • CHAPTER 5

beginner classes who had always filled in his workbook in and out of class in spite of long hours of construction work that resulted in him speaking in an exhausted, though warm, tone.

The advanced class was mainly men in their twenties and had been together for a couple years, so I could see their class being a difficult one to join. Rosa and Gerald joined the class and remained in it, perhaps because Rosa had grown children and was not intimidated, while Gerald studied hard, which no doubt earned the respect of the advanced students who did not want to slow down for new students. Mercedes was one of my smartest students who wanted to go on to the advanced class but returned to the intermediate group. She asked questions and helped the older Elena who sat next to her and occasionally looked at Mercedes's workbook or asked for an explanation in Spanish. I was glad to have Mercedes for the additional explanations with her fellow students, although I felt uncomfortable that she might have been able to move on to the next level but had returned.

LITERACY, WANTING TO LEARN, AND ACCESS

Jackie's comment that students don't seem to want to move on speaks to a dominant narrative that because Indigenous Latin American migrants come from poverty, they automatically do not know about education and whether they need it. Valenzuela makes an important point about how students who migrate to the US do in fact care about education and can oftentimes actually perform better than US-born Mexican American students who have internalized the experience of marginalization as a "minority": "Immigrant students acquiesce. Their grounded sense of identity combines with the unfamiliarity of the Mexican minority experience to enable them to 'care about' school without the threat of language or culture loss" (24). Caring is one thing, but caring without access only serves to blame the victim of the discriminatory educational policy. As early as 1998, rhetoricians have called attention to the impact of racist policy on education in California: "In November 1994, more than two thirds of California's voters approved Proposition 187, an initiative aimed at denying health care, education, and other public services to undocumented immigrants" (Hasian and Delgado 253). By denying education to undocumented migrants, the xenophobic logic followed that this proposition would not have negative repercussions on the infrastructure of the state and its inhabitants because Latinx migrants, legal migrants, and US-born Latinx citizens did not care about education. Subtle changes like the increase in rates for "out-of-state" students, though less overtly discriminatory, continue along this xenophobic logic of exclusion.

The English classes at the Sanctuary came from a demand, or felt need, from within the community. However, with the English language program comes some of the pitfalls of literacy education. That the students recognized issues of class size and frequency showed this student population's awareness of what contributes to effective learning in spite of the predominantly manual labor jobs they perform. In "Cultivating Land-Based Literacies and Rhetorics," Gabriela Ríos references an advocate for campesino farmworkers who explains how traditional literacies are equated with intelligence and how farmworkers are therefore considered less intelligent because of the kind of work they do. Following a counterstory argument that resists stereotypical stock stories, Ríos quotes an advocate who explains, "People think that because Indigenous or poor and uneducated people do this work, that the work lacks intellect or skill. People assume that 'anyone' can do this form of labor because 'these people' can" (61). However, the advocate provides the counter perspective of many Indigenous farmworkers who have knowledge from the land: "But, we have skill. Many of us are Indigenous, and we have grown up knowing how to work with the land" (61). Guatemalan Maya receive education through the land: "Mayas receive their education in part through growing, preparing, and eating corn. . . . In the milpa too a young boy learns about the catastrophes of life, the vagaries of weather that can leave the family with too little food to survive in the coming year" (Green 18). In many ways the cost-prohibitive formal education Jackie advocated for was also out of alignment with more traditional education practices interconnected with remaining at a particular place and space.

With regard to literacy education, an underlying assumption of the English program at the Sanctuary undergirds the dominant narrative about campesino farmworkers needing literacy to improve themselves. Because their work is not associated with traditional reading and writing literacies, Ríos explains that "farm workers, many of whom are Latin@ and/or Mexican@, have similarly deployed rhetorics in response to ideologies of literacy that construct them as a-rhetorical" (60). From the perspective of the farmworkers she speaks with, they recognize how this dominant narrative about their literacy has a dehumanizing effect: "However well-intentioned—promoting traditional literacy as a universal tool of empowerment can have a dehumanizing effect on farm workers, especially those who do not speak a dominant language of power like English or Spanish" (61). While it was in fact the predominantly Indigenous Maya students who asked for more classes, the classes nevertheless perpetuated the idea of literacy as a universal tool of empowerment. The perspective of the farmworker advocate that Ríos speaks with comes from experience with many Indigenous campesino workers, though it might conflict with the suggestions of the students I spoke with at the Sanctuary because they have their

118 · CHAPTER 5

rhetorical sovereignty (Lyons; King), with rights to their own perspectives and arguments about literacy.

The work of campesino farmworkers might require less English literacy than urban jobs such as construction and housekeeping performed by students at the Sanctuary; either way, these competing perspectives about literacy from migrants speak to the diversity of perspectives counterstory facilitates. Perhaps because of Guatemala's high illiteracy rate, literacy as empowerment is a belief carried over from Guatemala when Indigenous Maya learn Spanish. Researcher Judith Zur describes a Maya woman who advocates for her children's education in Guatemala: "*Doña* Consuelo supported her husband's community work and agreed with his decision to send all their children to school, including girls. He recognized the advantages of a Spanish-language education in terms of job opportunities" (13). Spanish remains the language of colonial power in Central America and much of South America. In Guatemala, Indigenous Maya "men attempt to appropriate the power of the language they had learnt outside the community by sprinkling their conversation with Spanish words and phrases in order to impress or dominate fellow villagers" (32). While literacy might lead to more financial opportunities, Spanish language acquisition can also be a source of colonial power used against those who do not learn it, thereby setting the stage for resentment and disbelief in the value of plurilingualism.

While I respect Jackie's commitment to teaching at the Sanctuary, her frustration with the advanced students not wanting to move on follows the majoritarian narrative that these students do not know what is good for their education. It bears similarities with the dominant narrative Ríos identifies about campesino farmworkers doing manual labor due to a lack of intelligence (61). Misrepresenting manual laborers as less intelligent is an important narrative to bring to light because of its racist, classist, and ableist assumptions; what Jackie and those who promote more education without knowing Guatemalan history do not understand is that education made Maya into larger targets during their thirty-six year "civil war": "As mothers, women are ambivalent about the merits of education; they see its theoretical advantages but they also know that most rural, educated Indians were killed during *la violencia*" (Zur 33). The theoretical promise of literacy stands in stark contrast with the experiences of an Indigenous population, much like the Native boarding schools in the US and Canada where mass graves have been found reveal the historical dangers associated by Indigenous populations with education (Johnson).

While the classist, racist, and ableist assumptions about intelligence and labor are recognized by campesino farmworkers, the desire and feedback from the students at the Sanctuary evidence their ability to learn more than the volunteer teachers can provide. Perhaps Gerald agreeing with the feedback about the Sanctuary classes not covering enough new material affected me the most because he was by far one of the best students, having risen through the introductory and intermediate classes into the advanced class, *a feat accomplished by no other student*. Listening to the feedback of students like Gerald reinforces the work of Indigenous education scholars who say education is one of the important sites where Indigenous peoples' voices "must direct all the discussions about how best to achieve self-determination" (Deyhle et al., qtd. in Wane 162). The penciled-in pages of Gerald's workbook with answers in the blank spaces and translations written in the margins attest to limits of the standardized curriculum. In an interview, Gerald revealed he had children back at home in Guatemala, and learning English brings him closer to his goals of taking care of his family. While he might not be indicative of all the students at the Sanctuary, his story still speaks to how the measure of intelligence can be tacitly applied and rescinded to fit the needs of those who know "what's best" for migrant students.

Jackie's time as a volunteer teacher in the advanced class shows firsthand that she knew the students wanted to learn. However, her familiarity with the ease of access to additional classes highlights not just the lack of access but also the barriers to education white US citizens do not always recognize because it's often not a part of their lived experiences. One of the major issues for migrants who want to learn English is that the resources meant for communities tend to exclude these populations most vulnerable and in need of support. Community colleges in California provided limited access by charging an additional $211 per unit for "out-of-state" students on top of the in-state rate of $46 per unit ("Tuition and Fees"). Not only are these students asked to pay nearly 500 percent of what California residents pay, but they also continue to be targets of xenophobic rhetoric. Jackie's concern for the advanced students not moving on to other institutions demonstrates a key aspect of majoritarian stories. Majoritarian stories in education possess this quality that "begins from the assumption that all students enjoy access to the same educational opportunities and conditions from elementary through postsecondary school" (Yosso 4). That many of these students come from Guatemala, which has one of the lowest levels of literacy in Central America, shows how these students embrace education and make the most out of the resources afforded to them.

Writing studies and English language learning scholar Paul Kei Matsuda describes how treating students as though they all have the same linguistic background and privilege punishes those students who do not have access to the dominant variety of English. Matsuda writes, "Those who are not native speakers of dominant varieties of English are thus being held accountable for what is not being taught" (640). Migrants who seek refuge from poverty and high rates of homicide and unemployment find themselves expected to operate in spaces legislated by English-only policies without access to the English education that would allow them to do so. This is often the case for many English language learners who experience discrimination because of barriers to access: "ELLs access to higher level courses is limited along with their possibilities for college entrance" (Liggett 116). Even though Jackie might have had good intentions for students at the Sanctuary, her logic follows a majoritarian narrative that blames the students rather than acknowledging the underlying racial and economic discrimination operating within the educational system that enforces barriers to access.

DISTRUST IN AUTHORITY

That Carlos trusted Isabel and the church staff to call the police and give a statement speaks to the level of trust Carlos felt at the Sanctuary. Many migrants feel the vulnerability of being targeted due to citizenship status and prior negative experiences with governmental and legal authorities. When Trump characterized the caravans of migrants coming from Central America through Mexico as harboring MS-13 gang members and terrorists, he appealed to the ideological fear of the "immigrant as criminal" stock story. This stock story can be seen as having played out in much of US history when policy was written, as Derrick Bell explains, to protect white property ("Brown . . . Forty-Five Years" 175). This logic of white supremacy has been used to legally support the separation of families at the border and the locking up of children in cages (Southern Poverty Law Center). The stock story logic includes arguments such as "If they didn't do anything wrong, then they'd have no reason to be afraid of law enforcement." However, many of those targeted for deportation under the Obama administration were only guilty of having crossed the border, as opposed to belonging to gangs or having committed additional crimes (Ribero, "Citizenship" 38). For many, merely seeking refuge becomes their criminal offense.

Mateo told me that when the local police contacted the Sanctuary and wanted to meet with the Spanish-speaking congregation for community outreach, the attendance was low. Mateo cited fear and distrust. It is unfortunate that migrants from Guatemala seeking refuge in the US have to remain vigilant about violence not only from theft, robberies, and assaults but also from state-sanctioned actions in the form of over-policing by US immigration agencies and overzealous local law enforcement. In a recent study of youth violence in Guatemala City, "the police were widely perceived as both inefficient and untrustworthy, and were (together with maras) frequently identified in discussion groups as the most negative institution in both communities" (Winton, "Youth" 175). In the context of Trump's fearmongering rhetoric against Mexicans as criminals and the Central American caravan as full of MS-13 gang members, experiences in Guatemala and immigration enforcement in the US help explain why the student population at the Sanctuary would be fearful of police.

In the surveys at the Sanctuary, the majority of respondents said that "work opportunities in the US" and "jobs at home" were the main reasons for coming, with some noting "gang violence" and others preferring not to say. Those preferring not to answer seem indicative of fear or distrust, which is completely understandable. The jobs at home and work opportunities in the US seem redundant, but work opportunities in the US outnumbered no work at home, which might have to do with the potential for violence even when employed. In a story for National Public Radio, a reporter in Guatemala City explains how gangs extort bus drivers with the fear of death: "Armed gangs demand bribes from the drivers. Drivers who don't pay up often pay with their lives. More than 70 drivers have been killed already this year [2009] in Guatemala and the problem is especially bad in the capital, Guatemala City" (Beaubien). Even those with jobs feared extortion from the *maras,* which were often found in areas with few job opportunities.

While Winton points out how gangs in the capital of Guatemala City impact the ability of many youths to leave their homes, Indigenous campesinos experience a similar lack of options after being displaced from their lands by the government and drug cartels. An activist working with these displaced campesinos explains how the circumstances they face leave them without options: These are "people who have lost their land, who have been kicked off their land and are now wondering where in the fucking world they're going to plant their corn, their beans, their seeds. And when they find a place in the middle of nowhere they'll be accused of being narcos again, they'll be kicked out and left to beg" (O. Martínez, *History* 64). Indigenous rhetoric scholar Andrea Riley Mukavetz explains how when teaching decolonial theory and methods, she confronts dominant narratives about American Indians that include displacement. Mukavetz explains that "after we discuss the history of indigenous peoples of Ohio, we talk about the implications of the region's dominant narrative that American Indians willingly left the area when they were actually systematically and violently removed" (126). Similar systemic and violent removals of Indigenous Maya in Guatemala contribute to the caravans and unaccompanied minors arriving at the US border, where immigration policy punishes people who are left without options in their home countries.

CONCLUSION

A couple weeks after Carlos was assaulted, I arrived at the Sanctuary fifteen minutes before class. Isabel and Ana were setting up when Isabel told me, "The teacher for the advanced class isn't coming." Ana said, "The teacher just told us." In reality, I had known Jackie wasn't going to come.

At some point Jackie had said, "I have some cancerous cells on my forehead that I need to have removed and I won't be able to come for a few weeks."

Selfishly, I had hoped Jackie was not making the case for potentially not returning to teach. However, I understood the time commitment she had already made to the Sanctuary classes, much longer than many other teachers. There is a certain inherent irony when volunteering in that you can do it on a short-term basis and feel good about the minimal participation. The longer you are part of a volunteer project, the worse you feel leaving because you are more aware of what needs to continue to be done.

For Mateo, the birth of his first son provided him with the right reason to take a step back. As a part of his transition out of the English program, Mateo met with Isabel, Ana, and other staff who helped with the English program and operations. They discussed concerns and prioritized what should be emphasized amid changes in students and teachers. Their meeting concluded before a Monday evening prayer. In the basement, a large group of students had gathered, and I introduced myself to a couple of newer teachers I did not recognize.

I began to move a few of the basement tables to organize what would be the classroom area for the introductory level. One of the newer volunteers helped me. I didn't get his name, knowing that either he or I probably wouldn't last much longer. He explained that the two other English speakers I had introduced myself to were "working together to provide individualized attention to the members of the class."

I said, "There are a lot of signs from the school that operates out of the church reminding us to return the benches back to where they were."

This was not the proper response to the initiative of these new volunteers trying to provide individualized interactions. When I first started, I cotaught the introductory class with a young couple. The woman led the majority of the class, and I filled in where I could with her spouse, even though I had more teaching experience. She was well prepared and brought a lot of enthusiasm that more than made up for her lack of experience. By my third year at the Sanctuary, I valued the consistency of the volunteers more than dynamic pedagogies that burned bright like fireworks exploding in the sky, but which burned out and faded away from the Sanctuary just as quickly.

It is not my intention to portray Jackie as anything other than a volunteer teacher who became frustrated working within a racist system that blinded her from her privilege, though wanting more for her students. Racism is normalized through policy and laws misunderstood as neutral, and whiteness provides a protection and inclusion, away from the obstacles and barriers imposed on nonwhites. Jackie's feelings of frustration within Kafkaesque immigration and education systems conjure up the dominant narratives that often come in response to questions about inequality. Dominant narratives reinforce assumptions about there being a baseline of equality within systems rigged by policies based on the enduring legacies of colonialism and white supremacy in the US.

At the end of my time at the Sanctuary, I wondered about the fate of the Spanish-speaking congregation and its struggle over the lease with the English-speaking congregation. I wondered about my own commitment with two sons under the age of five, escalating job responsibilities, and the insecurity of the Sanctuary English program and lease.

•

On the night Jackie didn't show, after the prayer, Isabel looked at me and said, "You might be the only teacher here tonight. Can you teach the beginner class?"

The beginner class was always the largest, with the students occupying the majority of the basement.

"I'll get my things from my classroom upstairs," I said.

When I reached the top of the stairs, I poked my head into the other intermediate classroom that was not mine. I asked, "Is the teacher here?"

Students smiled and shook their heads "no." Ana, the other Sanctuary staff member, was standing at the front door of the Sanctuary, greeting students as they entered.

"Have you seen the other teachers?" I asked.

"Sí, estan aquí," she said. "No preoccupes." She pointed to a man with a ponytail entering the classroom where I had just poked my head inside.

I asked about the downstairs, and she said she would check on it. I was relieved a beginner class teacher was there and that I wouldn't have to combine my intermediate class with the beginner class.

Some of the advanced students began to gather around the entryway of the church as classes began. I passed out a worksheet on the correct uses of "to," "too," and "two." Because I had a few extra, I handed them to the students I know in the advanced class lingering outside my classroom. They each responded, "Thank you, teacher."

The desire of these students to learn is what kept me coming back over those three years. The strong community held together by Pastor Pablo and Isabel let me know that, even in my absence, the Sanctuary would continue to serve as a refuge where recent migrants could find the support and resources they needed. As recently as fall 2022, I was sitting at a table with first-generation college students at my institution, and when I learned that one of the students was from the East Bay, I let her know that I had taught at the Sanctuary church. The student's expression changed as she said to me, "My family goes to that church."

Without asking if her parents took part in the English program, I could still imagine the hours she spent there. She had no doubt studied in the low light of the basement or in a room adjacent to a band practicing or the men's group holding their weekly meetings. I was inspired to see her in the first-generation scholars program I taught in at a school where all of her hard work would be supported with resources. Without knowing the success stories of my former students, I can only put my hope against the hauntings for similar outcomes for their children.

CHAPTER 6

Concluding a Story without an End

Between the ages of five and eight, I spent a lot of time at my half-Guatemalan grandmother Dorothy's house. Her two-bedroom, one-and-a-half-bathroom house was around the corner from where I lived during elementary school, so I was brought there or told to walk there after school days when my parents were working late or when my mother was taking classes for her TESOL (teaching English as a second language) degree. One day when I was six, my grandmother told me to practice writing my name in cursive, but when I wrote my name so big that it filled the entire page, she lectured me to no end about how I "write big" and "want to act like a grown-up." Her lecturing skills had been sharpened from having raised four children of her own. My aunt and uncles always told me that I got the "nice" version of my grandma, not like the one they had growing up as kids. The secrecy around how my grandmother parentalized, terrorized, and manipulated my father, aunt, and uncles silenced the notion that there was any other version of a woman who lashed out because of her traumas. My "nice" version of grandma took part in a weekly recovery group she had become active in after having a "breakdown" when she was younger. My "nice" grandma read self-help books about healing by Louis Hay. I can only imagine my grandmother's time spent healing, like my own time in therapy, as an attempt to address generational trauma. But therapy also teaches us that there are not always easy answers, and you have to confront what you have learned to avoid.

126 · CHAPTER 6

For this book, I would like to believe I answered the questions I set out to, although I recognize that my questions and lines of inquiry had to change based on what I learned about the migrant student population and how much more I wanted to learn from them. Even as I sought out to inquire about the American Dream and what it meant in the shifting political landscape, I was well aware of how it should be critically regarded as a myth and a point of departure into other reasons the US continues to be a destination for refuge from places where violence is a lived reality. However, in my interactions with this migrant student population, I was reminded of how each generation of migrants reconstitutes what their American Dream is, and much like democracy, it might be a humble hope for something better. It is something that is struggled for in an attempt to make it a reality.

I am indebted to the scholarship on Guatemala and the genocide rewritten in political narratives as "civil war" in order to assuage the United States' culpability. I am grateful for the boots-on-the-ground journalism and research on narco-trafficking violence that is no less brutal as the best and worst example of unbridled capitalism. Without this work, I could not have gotten into the depths of learned silence as a survival strategy that colonial narratives might continue to misinterpret as stereotypical beliefs about "stoic Natives" or Native people lacking knowledge. Indeed, in this concluding chapter, I feel the necessary presence through the haunting absence of what my students did and did not say because this silence speaks for the trauma no families should have to endure.

At the end of my time at the Sanctuary, I wanted more closure. I somewhat naively wanted a happy ending promising sustained health, safety, and social mobility for everyone at the Sanctuary. Instead, following the events of the book came the signing of executive orders by Trump that led to 5,400 children being separated from their parents at the US border during the Trump administration: "More than 2,100 children" had yet to be reunited with their parents (Soboroff). These mass separations of migrants from their children at the border came as a result of Trump's "zero tolerance" executive action. This broad, sweeping racist policy that tore apart families leaves many more migrants seeking asylum. Most stories of immigration do not have convenient conclusions. Relying on the status quo of "that's just our old broken immigration system" is what continues to allow gender-based violence to continue without protections or accountability.

There are always many intertwined lived experiences with traumas that can be difficult, if impossible, to recover from. Perhaps the use of scene and story suggests the expectation of a conclusive ending about the future of the Sanctuary church or what happened to the English-speaking congregation. But as much as we endeavor to present the responses to surveys, interviews, and observations in some kind of cohesive piece of writing, we need to acknowledge the messiness of research that involves the lives of community members that cannot be contained or whose stories we only see and hear glimpses of.

(UN)ANSWERED RESEARCH QUESTIONS

At the beginning of this research in 2013, I sought to learn more about the intersections of race, citizenship, and language through the research site of a Spanish-speaking church where I volunteered to teach English to migrant students predominantly from Guatemala. My concerns about race came from living and studying in Arizona, where the "papers please" SB 1070 law had been passed that called the citizenship of all Latinxs into question, while at the same time House Bill 2281 outlawed Mexican American studies in the Tucson School District, making Indigenous and Latinx knowledge illegitimate. With copycat legislation appearing in states like Alabama, I feared the widespread adoption of ultraconservative politics could become a reality. As Trump campaigned during my time at the Sanctuary, his brand of ultraconservative racism was becoming more mainstream. Like a lot of US Americans, I couldn't believe so many voters would tacitly approve of his racism for whatever snake-oil promises Trump had sold them about coal jobs and building a wall.

This research began shortly after I moved to Santa Clara, California, where I wanted to learn more about this affluent area that was difficult to live in on a postdoctoral fellowship. Chapter 1 began with the migrant student's question of "How can you help me?" alongside Pope Francis's criticism of free market capitalism, perhaps because I was struggling to cover rent and childcare, so I knew the migrant students were feeling it much harder. My goal with this first chapter was to trace the tradition of exclusion in the idealized state of California, which Hollywood might have you believe is all beachfront property and liberal politics. This chapter provides further exigency for rethinking the United States' role in global migration in part because of an entrenched belief in free market capitalism. With the perils of social media coming to the forefront, the tech industry of Silicon Valley will never be thought of as being as seemingly harmless and full of potential as it once was; instead, the neoliberal boosterism of the Bay Area that championed Silicon Valley as bringing the world together will have the roots of capitalism and colonialism unearthed in what might contribute to the larger project of returning land to Indigenous populations.

In chapter 2 I posit tenets for bringing together decolonial methodology and critical race theory because colonialism relies on instituting socially constructed differences, including racism, to conquer and spread ideologies across space and time. Since 2020, and with the heightened attention to issues of racism because of the murders of Black men and women, including George Floyd and Breonna Taylor, the awareness of the permanence of racism has been more widespread. This awareness prompted many to consider the possibility of new worlds and realities that exist outside of racial hierarchies. Still, I respect those who might disagree with what I posit because their lived experiences with most anything related to "diversity" and "inclusivity" have been limited to empty promises and institutional statements that have done little to make any real change in the world.

When consulting colleagues about chapters, one of the questions I got about chapter 3 was why I did not include more primary research on sexual assault. Sexual violence was not explicit in my preliminary research about race, citizenship, language, and property. As the motivations for migration began to reveal the strategies of silence practiced by the adult students, I still felt it was within my role as their English language teacher to push beyond the areas I asked about in surveys. I entered the Sanctuary as an educator first before asking permission to conduct research, so I never wanted to do anything as a researcher that could impact my role as an educator.

In chapter 3 I reference the sexual assault I learned about from a survivor while in Mexico; this migrant woman shared her experience of having been sexually assaulted by a US Border Patrol officer, which she recounted while I was a participant in a Jesuit immersion trip with my university. I visited a Jesuit food distribution site where migrants were asked to share their experiences with the visitors preparing and serving the food. After I had cut vegetables and handed out plates of food, our group was invited to hear from different migrants in different stages of having been deported and crossing over. The survivor of the sexual assault shared her experience as we listened in small groups of two and three to many of the migrants' stories. I spoke with a mother in her forties with children in Georgia she was trying to get back to in the face of further legal restrictions. I listened to a woman forced to join a gang when she got locked up after being caught crossing over. I spoke with a young man who grew up undocumented in the US but who got into trouble with drugs and was deported, even though his experiences were the same as those of many documented US citizens. All of these people asked that we share their stories so the issue of immigration could have a human face.

The topic of language in chapter 4 is perhaps one of the most explicit connections with the original research I thought I might learn more about when I began this project. What I did not know was that in addition to my speaking with the students about language learning, the Sanctuary church would

CONCLUDING A STORY WITHOUT AN END · 129

undergo a struggle over the lease with linguistic differences used against the staff and members. Just as mysteriously as the English-speaking church was somehow able to sign the lease for the property both the Sanctuary and their church occupied, the issue with the lease resolved itself. When I concluded my time at the beginning of summer 2016, there was lingering concern and little tangible resolution about the future of the Sanctuary, beyond the unproductive meetings where Mateo had served as translator. When I ran into one of the other volunteer teachers by chance at birthdays for Mateo's children (he now has four little boys), we would inevitably circle back to the Sanctuary with some nostalgia and strange unsettled exchanges about the somewhat mysterious end to the lease struggle, which had been such a focal point for so many of the Monday prayer sessions. Not speaking as a researcher, I would say that perhaps prayers do, in fact, work. Or maybe the lack of works performed by the English-speaking congregation brought about its own end. As Nielly, one of the other volunteer teachers and a pastor at a different church, and I had both observed, there never seemed to be anyone at the English-speaking church building while we were there. When the English-speaking church signed the lease and kept the Sanctuary church in a state of peril, it might have been a last-ditch effort on their part to grab for some power, very well knowing that the end of their church was near.

Chapter 5 set out to offer a counterstory that brought together the initial topics in a way that helped to address how racist policy impacts language education in relation to citizenship status and dominant narratives about what is wanted from migrants (i.e., learn the language). While I did not set out to underscore how racism impacts even the narratives implied by other volunteer teachers, the first tenet of CRT reminds us how racism circulates through all our realities. I hope the counterstory also offered my own humanity and messy role as a burned-out volunteer in a program that received no local or state funding, and perhaps provokes some sympathy for those educators in public institutions trying to help students pulled in multiple directions by work, family, and concerns about citizenship. I hope that all educators continue to have students who inspire them to return. I wish that both students and teachers get the resources and support they deserve and need to make education accessible for those who want and need it.

CONCLUSION

As a part of the reflective practice that decolonial methodologies emphasize as a part of the messiness of researching within research sites complicit with colonial paradigms, I return to Godwin Agboka, who notes that "it is difficult to adjust the design to accommodate local situations" (301). From my experiences in Arizona with its racist anti-Latinx policy, I entered into the Sanctuary as a researcher with an interest in the impacts of racism in the Bay Area and how it affected the lived experiences of this migrant population. Instead, I reveal the racism and anti-Indigenous violence outside of the US that precipitates migration to the US, where the memories of violence and corruption continue impacting the daily lives of people who exist in precarious, liminal spaces as potentially disposable labor and who feel outside the protection of the legal system. In wanting to learn more about the intersection of race and language for Indigenous migrants, I learned more about how the US continues benefiting from silencing voices abroad through the tacit support of terror campaigns launched against Indigenous populations to maintain supply chains.

By 2016 Mateo's missionary organization required he and his family to take a sabbatical from his work as a part of their standard rotation procedures. Mateo's sabbatical served as a somewhat clear date for me to conclude volunteering, as it would come at the end of a class term at the Sanctuary. Perhaps if I lived closer to the Sanctuary church, I would have been less worn down by the commute and would have stayed longer. Perhaps if I had sought out a grant to secure funding for the program to guarantee sustained support? What if the US didn't rely on volunteer programs to educate the people they rely on for labor? Questions for absent authorities echoing unanswered haunt the colonized and show exigency for imagining new worlds.

Since my volunteer work at the Mission ended, Trump's presidency has also concluded, and Joe Biden has continued to uphold Trump-era anti-immigrant policy. My grandma Dorothy's husband, my grandpa Julian, didn't survive Trump, dying in 2020, though cancer at age ninety-seven was more of the cause. Since her first stroke in 2010, my grandma Dorothy's health has continued to decline and her powerful voice that echoes throughout my memories of writing my name in cursive has quieted to a low murmur. Mateo serves as a missionary with his wife Martha in Modesto, California. And the Sanctuary church continues offering assistance to new migrants in the East Bay, doing what it can to make the difficult transition from painful circumstances easier, even if only a bit.

APPENDIX

Survey Questions

PREGUNTAS DE LA ENCUESTA

1. Cual es su edad?
   a. 18–25 años
   b. 26–35 años
   c. 36–45 años
   d. 46 años o mas
   e. Prefiero no contestar

2. De cual paiz es usted?
   a. Mexico
   b. Guatemala
   c. Honduras
   d. El Salvador
   e. Prefiero no contestar

3. Por cuantos años estaba en los EE. UU.?
   a. 1–2 años
   b. 3–4 años
   c. 5–9 años
   d. 10 años o mas
   e. Prefiero no contestar

4. Por cuantos años esta aprendiendo ingles?
   a. 0–1 años
   b. 2–3 años
   c. 3–4 años
   d. 5 o mas años
   e. Prefiero no contestar

5. Porque venio usted a los EE. UU.? (Haga circulo por todos que applican.)
   a. Oportunidades para trabajo
   b. Violencia de los pandilla
   c. Familia en los EE UU
   d. No trabajo en su pais
   e. Prefiero no contestar

6. Si usted ha sido víctima de discriminación, era más probable debido a: (Marque todo lo que corresponda.)
   a. Raza latina
   b. Las creencias negativas sobre los inmigrantes
   c. Clase económica
   d. Habilidad para hablar Inglés
   e. Prefiere no contestar

7. ¿Qué piensa usted acerca de las leyes de inmigración en los EE. UU.? (Marque todas las que apliquen.)
   a. Demasiado confuse
   b. Demasiados
   c. Dañan latinos.
   d. Me duelen todas las familias inmigrantes.
   e. Prefiere no contestar

8. ¿Cómo funciona el sonido noticias del periódico o la televisión cuando se habla de inmigración? (Encerrar en un círculo.)
   a. Positivo
   b. Neutral
   c. Negativo
   d. No seguro
   e. Prefiere no contestar

9. ¿Qué opinas sobre el Sueño Americano ? (Marque todas las que apliquen.)
   a. Es posible.
   b. Es difícil de lograr.
   c. Es imposible de lograr.
   d. No existe.
   e. Prefiere no contestar

10. ¿Hay un problema con el racismo en los EE. UU.?
   a. Si
   b. No
   c. Prefiere no contestar

11. La televisión y los periódicos historias sobre los latinos y los inmigrantes latinos: (Marque todas las que aplican.)
   a. Por lo general, verdadera
   b. Parcialmente cierto
   c. Decir mentiras
   d. Dicen cosas negativas sobre los latinos y los inmigrantes
   e. Prefiere no contestar

12. Si usted está interesado en hablar más con el Dr. Cruz Medina en un pequeño grupo sobre las preguntas y cuestiones en esta encuesta, por favor escriba su nombre y él se comunicará con usted: _____.
   (Todos los nombres serán retirados de las encuestas después de su recolección.)

SURVEY QUESTIONS

1. What is your age?
   a. 18–25 years old
   b. 26–35 years old
   c. 36–45 years old
   d. 46 years or older
   e. Prefer not to answer

2. What country are you from?
   a. Mexico
   b. Guatemala
   c. Honduras
   d. El Salvador
   e. Prefer not to answer

3. How long have you been in the US?
   a. 1–2 years
   b. 3–4 years
   c. 5–9 years
   d. 10 years or more
   e. Prefer not to answer

4. How many years have you been learning English?
   a. 0–1 year
   b. 2–3 years
   c. 3–4 years
   d. 5 or more years
   e. Prefer not to answer

5. Why did you come to the US? (Circle all that apply.)
   a. Work opportunities
   b. Gang violence at home
   c. Family in the US
   d. No jobs at home
   e. Prefer not to answer

APPENDIX • 135

6. If you have experienced discrimination, it was most likely because of: (Circle all that apply.)
   a. Race as Latino
   b. Negative beliefs about immigrants
   c. Economic class
   d. Ability to speak English
   e. Prefer not to answer

7. What do you think about the immigration laws in the US? (Circle all that apply.)
   a. Too confusing
   b. Too many
   c. They harm Latinos.
   d. They hurt all immigrant families.
   e. Prefer not to answer

8. How does the newspaper or television news sound when talking about immigration? (Circle only one.)
   a. Positive
   b. Neutral
   c. Negative
   d. Unsure
   e. Prefer not to answer

9. What do you think about the American Dream? (Circle all that apply.)
   a. It is possible.
   b. It is difficult to achieve.
   c. It is impossible to achieve.
   d. It does not exist.
   e. Prefer not to answer

10. Is there a problem with racism in the US?
   a. Yes
   b. No
   c. Prefer not to answer

11. Television and newspaper stories about Latinos and Latino immigrants: (Circle all that apply.)
    a. Usually true
    b. Mostly true
    c. Tell lies
    d. Say negative things about Latinos and immigrants
    e. Prefer not to answer

12. If you are interested in talking more with Dr. Cruz Medina in a small group about the questions and issues in this survey, please write your name and he will contact you: _____. (All names will be removed from surveys after they are collected.)

WORKS CITED

Acuña, Rodolfo. *Occupied America. The Chicano's Struggle Toward Liberation.* 4th ed., Longman, 2000.

Agboka, Godwin Y. "Decolonial Methodologies: Social Justice Perspectives in Intercultural Technical Communication Research." *Journal of Technical Writing and Communication,* vol. 44, no. 3, 2014, pp. 297–327.

Alexander, Michelle. *The New Jim Crow: Mass Incarceration in the Age of Colorblindness.* The New Press, 2012.

Alvarez, Steven. *Brokering Tareas: Mexican Immigrant Families Translanguaging Homework Literacies.* SUNY Press, 2017.

———. "Rhetorical Autoethnography: Delinking English Language Learning in a Family Oral History." *Rhetorics Elsewhere and Otherwise: Contested Modernities, Decolonial Visions,* edited by Romeo Garcia and Damián Baca, Studies in Writing and Rhetoric, National Council of Teachers of English, 2019, pp. 85–111.

American Civil Liberties Union. "ACLU Attorneys React to Argument at Supreme Court on Arizona's Anti-Immigrant Law." *ACLU San Diego and Imperial Counties,* 25 Apr. 2012, https://www.aclu-sdic.org/en/news/aclu-attorneys-react-argument-supreme-court-arizonas-anti-immigrant-law.

Anguiano, Claudia A. "Dropping the 'I-Word': A Critical Examination of Contemporary Immigration Labels." *The Rhetorics of US Immigration: Identity, Community and Otherness,* edited by Johanna E. Hartelius, Penn State UP, 2015, pp. 93–111.

Anzaldúa, Gloria. *Borderlands/La Frontera: The New Mestiza.* Spinster / Aunt Lute Books, 1987.

"AP Explains: The Growing Migrant Caravan on Way to US Border." *Associated Press,* 22 Oct. 2018, https://apnews.com/article/central-america-us-news-ap-top-news-honduras-immigration-09e3fc70d338418e849ffee13712c2a3.

138 · WORKS CITED

Arana, Ana. "How the Street Gangs Took Central America." *Foreign Affairs,* vol. 84, no. 3, 2005, pp. 98–110. *JSTOR,* https://doi.org/10.2307/20034353.

Arellano, Sonia C. "Sexual Violences Traveling to El Norte: An Example of Quilting as Method." *College Composition and Communication,* vol. 72, no. 4, 2021, pp. 500–515.

Balzac, Honoré de. "Le Père Goriot." *Revue de Paris,* vol. 12, 1834.

Baker-Bell, April. *Linguistic Justice: Black Language, Literacy, Identity, and Pedagogy.* Routledge, 2020.

Bean, John, editor. *The Ohlone Past and Present: Native Americans of the San Francisco Bay Region.* Bellena, 1994.

Beaubien, Jason. "Crime, Corruption Killing Guatemalan Bus Drivers." *Morning Edition,* 4 June 2009, https://www.npr.org/2009/06/04/104922411/crime-corruption-killing-guatemalan-bus-drivers.

Bell, Derrick. "Brown v. Board of Education: Forty-Five Years after the Fact." *Ohio Northern University Law Review,* vol. 26, no. 2, 2000, pp. 171–82.

Bell, Derrick A. "Brown v. Board of Education and the Interest-Convergence Dilemma." *Harvard Law Review,* vol. 93, no. 3, 1980, pp. 518–33. *JSTOR,* https://doi.org/10.2307/1340546.

Bell, Derrick A., Jr. "Serving Two Masters: Integration Ideals and Client Interests in School Desegregation Litigation." *Yale Law Journal,* vol. 85, no. 4, Mar. 1976, pp. 470–517.

Bonilla-Silva, Eduardo. "Toward a New Political Praxis for Trumpamerica: New Directions in Critical Race Theory." *American Behavioral Scientist,* vol. 63, no. 13, Nov. 2019, pp. 1776–88. *Sage Journals,* https://doi.org/10.1177/0002764219842614.

Bose, Purnima. "Kamala Harris's *The Truths We Hold*: An American Journey." *American Literary History,* vol. 32 no. 2, 2020, pp. e25–e32. *Project MUSE,* https://muse.jhu.edu/article/762157.

Cedillo, Christina V. "Disabled and Undocumented: In/Visibility at the Borders of Presence, Disclosure, and Nation." *Rhetoric Society Quarterly,* vol. 50, no. 3, 2020, pp. 203–11. *Taylor & Francis Online,* https://doi.org/10.1080/02773945.2020.1752131.

Chávez, Karma R. "Beyond Inclusion: Rethinking Rhetoric's Historical Narrative." *Quarterly Journal of Speech,* vol. 101, no. 1, 2015, pp. 162–72.

Chávez-Moreno, Laura C. "Researching Latinxs, Racism, and White Supremacy in Bilingual Education: A Literature Review." *Critical Inquiry in Language Studies,* vol. 17, no. 2, 2020, pp. 101–20.

Cintron, Ralph. *Angels' Town: Chero Ways, Gang Life, and Rhetorics of the Everyday.* Beacon Press, 1997.

Cisneros, Josue D. *The Border Crossed Us: Rhetorics of Borders, Citizenship, and Latina/o Identity.* U of Alabama P, 2014.

Commission for Historical Clarification. "Guatemala—Memory of Silence: Report of the Commission for Historical Clarification: Conclusions and Recommendations (February 1999)." *Die Friedens-Warte,* vol. 74, no. 4, Berliner Wissenschafts-Verlag, 1999, pp. 511–47. *JSTOR,* https://www.jstor.org/stable/23778631.

Cortez, José M. "From a Community Yet to Arrive." *Working-Class Rhetorics,* edited by Jennifer Beech and Matthew Wayne Guy, Brill, 2021, pp. 39–43, Critical Media Literacies Series 9, https://doi.org/10.1163/9789004501508_004.

Crawford, James. *At War with Diversity: US Language Policy in an Age of Anxiety.* Multilingual Matters, 2002.

Crenshaw, Kimberlé W. "Race, Reform, and Retrenchment: Transformation and Legitimation in Antidiscrimination Law." *Harvard Law Review,* vol. 101, no. 7, 1988, pp. 1331–87.

Cushman, Ellen, Damián Baca, and Romeo García. "Delinking: Toward Pluriversal Rhetorics." *College English,* vol. 84, no. 1, 2021, pp. 7–32.

WORKS CITED • 139

Delgado, Richard. "Brewer's Plea: Critical Thoughts on Common Cause." *Vanderbilt Law Review,* vol. 44, no. 1, 1991, pp. 1–14.

Delgado, Richard, and Jean Stefancic. *Critical Race Theory: An Introduction.* 2nd ed., New York UP, 2012.

Demo, Anne Teresa. "Faithful Sovereignty: Denationalizing Immigration Policy in the 2003 Pastoral Letter on Migration." *The Rhetorics of US Immigration: Identity, Community, Otherness,* edited by Johanna E. Hartelius, Penn State UP, 2015, pp. 50–52.

Driskill, Qwo-Li. "Decolonial Skillshares: Indigenous Rhetorics as Radical Practice." *Survivance, Sovereignty, and Story: Teaching American Indian Rhetorics,* edited by Lisa King et al., Utah State UP, 2015, pp. 57–78.

"El Salvador's 677 Murders in June Most Since Civil War." *Associated Press,* 3 July 2015, https://apnews.com/article/cb0b9c0fde0648c98a8a897f0665ea34.

Elassar, Alaa. "University Launches Investigation after a Black Professor Was Asked by Campus Security to Prove She Lived in Her Own House." *CNN,* 26 Aug. 2020, https://www.cnn.com/2020/08/24/us/santa-clara-university-black-professor-campus-security-trnd/index.html.

England, Nora C. *A Grammar of Mam, a Mayan Language.* U of Texas P, 1983.

England, Sarah. *Writing Terror on the Bodies of Women: Media Coverage of Violence against Women in Guatemala.* Rowman & Littlefield, 2018.

Escobar, Arturo. *Designs for the Pluriverse: Radical Interdependence, Autonomy, and the Making of Worlds.* Duke UP, 2017. *JSTOR,* http://www.jstor.org/stable/j.ctv11smgs6.

Espinosa-Aguilar, Amanda. "Illegal." *Decolonizing Rhetoric and Composition Studies: New Latinx Keywords for Theory and Pedagogy,* edited by Iris D. Ruiz and Raúl Sánchez, Palgrave Macmillan, 2016, pp. 155–68.

Field, Delbert H., Jr. "Migration Management Challenges in Guatemala." *IOM UN Migration,* 21 Sept. 2012, https://weblog.iom.int/migration-management-challenges-guatemala.

Field, Les W. "Unacknowledged Tribes, Dangerous Knowledge: The Muwekma Ohlone and How Indian Identities Are 'Known.'" *Wicazo Sa Review,* vol. 18 no. 2, 2003, pp. 79–94. *Project MUSE,* https://doi.org/10.1353/wic.2003.0012.

Flores, Lisa A. *Deportable and Disposable: Public Rhetoric and the Making of the "Illegal" Immigrant.* Penn State UP, 2020.

Francis, Pope. *Evangelii Gaudium (The Joy of the Gospel).* The Word Among Us Press, 2013.

García, Ofelia. "Education, Multilingualism and Translanguaging in the 21st Century." *Social Justice through Multilingual Education,* edited by Tove Skutnabb-Kangas et al., Multilingual Matters, 2009, pp. 140–58.

García, Romeo. "Haunt (ed/ing) Genealogies and Literacies." *Reflections: A Journal of Public Rhetoric, Civic Writing & Service Learning,* vol. 19, no. 1, 2019, pp. 230–52.

Garcia, Ruben J. "Critical Race Theory and Proposition 187: The Racial Politics of Immigration Law (Comment)." *Chicano-Latino Law Review,* vol. 17, no. 118, 1995, pp. 118–54.

García Martínez, Antonio. *Chaos Monkeys: Obscene Fortune and Random Failure in Silicon Valley.* Harper Collins Publishers, 2016.

Glaser, B. G. "Grounded Theory Is the Study of a Concept!" *YouTube,* uploaded by jillrhine, 2010, https://www.youtube.com/watch?v=OcpxaLQDnLk.

Gonzales, Laura. *Sites of Translation: What Multilinguals Can Teach Us about Digital Writing and Rhetoric.* Michigan UP, 2018.

Gordon, Raymond G., Jr. *Ethnologue: Languages of the World.* 15th ed., SIL International, 2005.

Green, Linda. *Fear as a Way of Life: Mayan Widows in Rural Guatemala.* Columbia UP, 1999.

Guatemalan Academy of Mayan Languages/Academia de Lenguas Mayas de Guatemala. *Pujb'il Yol Mam: Vocabulario Mam.* 2003.

Guerra, Juan. *Close to Home: Oral and Literate Practices in a Transnational Mexicano Community.* Teachers College Columbia UP, 1998.

Gzesh, Susan. "Central Americans and Asylum Policy in the Reagan Era." *Migration Policy Institute,* 1 Apr. 2006, https://www.migrationpolicy.org/article/central-americans-and-asylum-policy-reagan-era.

Haas, Angela. "Toward a Decolonial Digital and Visual American Indian Rhetorics Pedagogy." *Survivance, Sovereignty, and Story: Teaching American Indian Rhetorics,* edited by Lisa King et al., Utah State UP, 2015, pp. 188–208.

Harris, Cheryl I. "Whiteness as Property." *Harvard Law Review,* vol. 106, no. 8, 1993, pp. 1707–91. *JSTOR,* https://doi.org/10.2307/1341787.

Hartelius, E. Johanna, editor. *The Rhetorics of US Immigration: Identity, Community, Otherness.* Penn State UP, 2015.

Hasian, Marouf, Jr., and Fernando Delgado. "The Trials and Tribulations of Racialized Critical Rhetorical Theory: Understanding the Rhetorical Ambiguities of Proposition 187." *Communication Theory,* vol. 8, no. 3, 1998, pp. 245–70, https://doi.org/10.1111/j.1468-2885.1998.tb00221.x.

Hayden, Tyler. "Number of Franciscan Priests Accused of Abuse Grows by Nine: New Report Shows Some Were Assigned to Santa Barbara after Allegations Elsewhere." *Santa Barbara Independent,* 5 June 2019, https://www.independent.com/2019/06/05/number-of-franciscan-priests-accused-of-abuse-grows-by-nine/.

Heidenreich, Linda. "Foreign Miners' Tax (1850)." *Latino History and Culture: An Encyclopedia,* edited by Pedro Malavet, Routledge, 2015, pp. 194–95.

Holmes, Ashley. *Public Pedagogy in Composition Studies.* National Council of Teachers of English, 2016.

Horner, Bruce, et al. "Language Difference in Writing: Toward a Translingual Approach." *College English,* vol. 73, no. 3, 2011, pp. 303–21. *JSTOR,* https://www.jstor.org/stable/25790477.

Ironside, Emily, and Lisa M. Corrigan. "Constituting Enemies through Fear." *The Rhetorics of US Immigration: Identity, Community, Otherness,* edited by Johanna E. Hartelius, Penn State UP, 2015, pp. 157–82.

Itchuaqiyaq, Cana Uluak, and Breeanne Matheson. "Decolonizing Decoloniality: Considering the (Mis)use of Decolonial Frameworks in TPC Scholarship." *Communication Design Quarterly,* vol. 9, no. 1, 2021, pp. 20–31.

Johnson, Bert. "The U.S. Interior Seeks to Reveal the Abusive Legacy of Indigenous Boarding Schools." *All Things Considered,* 10 Aug. 2021, https://www.npr.org/2021/08/10/1026500558/the-u-s-interior-seeks-to-reveal-the-abusive-legacy-of-indigenous-boarding-schoo.

Joint Venture Silicon Valley. *Silicon Valley Index.* Silicon Valley Institute for Regional Studies, 2014.

"Kamala Harris Tells Guatemala Migrants: Do Not Come to US." *BBC,* 7 June 2021, https://bbc.com/news/world-us-canada-57387350.

Kang, Cecilia, and Todd Frankel. "Silicon Valley Struggles to Hack Its Diversity Problem." *Washington Post,* 16 July 2016, https://www.washingtonpost.com/business/economy/silicon-valley-struggles-to-hack-its-diversity-problem/2015/07/16/0b0144be-2053-11e5-84d5-eb37ee8eaa61_story.html.

WORKS CITED · 141

Kessler, Glenn, et al. "Trump's False or Misleading Claims Total 30,573 over 4 Years." *Washington Post,* 24 Jan. 2021, https://washingtonpost.com/politics/2021/01/24/trumps-false-or-misleading-claims-total-30573-over-four-years.

King, Lisa. "Rhetorical Sovereignty and Rhetorical Alliance in the Writing Classroom: Using American Indian Texts." *Pedagogy,* vol. 12, no. 2, 2012, pp. 209–33.

King, Lisa, et al., editors. *Survivance, Sovereignty, and Story: Teaching American Indian Rhetorics.* Utah State UP, 2015.

Koh, Yoree. "Study: Immigrants Founded 51% of U.S. Billion-Dollar Startups." *Wall Street Journal,* 17 May 2016, https:// blogs.wsj.com/digits/2016/03/17/study-immigrants-founded-51-of-u-s-billion-dollar-startups/.

Kynard, Carmen. "Teaching While Black: Witnessing Disciplinary Whiteness, Racial Violence, and Race-Management." *Literacy in Composition Studies,* vol. 3, no. 1, 2015, pp. 1–20.

Ladson-Billings, Gloria, and William F. Tate. "Toward a Critical Race Theory of Education." *Teachers College Record,* vol. 97, no. 1, Sept. 1995, pp. 47–68. *Sage Journals,* https://doi.org/10.1177/016146819509700104.

Legg, Emily M. *Listening to Our Stories in Dusty Boxes: Indigenous Storytelling Methodology, Archival Practice, and the Cherokee Female Seminary.* 2016. Purdue U, PhD dissertation.

Leventhal, Alan, et al. "Back from Extinction: A Brief Overview of the Historic Disenfranchisement of the Ohlone Indian Peoples." *The Ohlones: Past and Present,* edited by Lowell J. Bean, Ballena, 1994, pp. 297–336.

Lewis, M. Paul, et al., editors. *Ethnologue: Languages of the World.* 18th ed., SIL International, 2015, https://www.ethnologue.com. Accessed 26 Aug. 2015.

Liggett, Tonda. "The Mapping of a Framework: Critical Race Theory and TESOL." *The Urban Review,* vol. 46, no. 1, 2014, pp. 112–24. *Springer Link,* https://doi.org/10.1007/s11256-013-0254-5.

Lloyd, Jens. "I Never Intended It to Become a Symbol of Resistance: An Interview with Xavier Maciel about the Sanctuary Campus Movement." *Reflections: A Journal of Community-Engaged Writing and Rhetoric,* vol. 18, no. 2, 2018/2019, pp. 151–65.

Lu, Min-Zhan. "Professing Multiculturalism: The Politics of Style in the Contact Zone." *College Composition and Communication,* vol. 45, no. 4, 1994, pp. 442–58. *JSTOR,* https://doi.org/10.2307/358759.

Lueck, Amy J., et al. "Public Memory as Community-Engaged Writing: Composing Difficult Histories on Campus." *Community Literacy Journal,* vol. 15, no. 2, 2021, pp. 9–30. *Digital Commons,* https://doi.org/10.25148/CLJ.15.2.009618.

Luibhéid, Eithne. "Introduction: Queering Migration and Citizenship." *Queer Migrations: Sexuality, U.S. Citizenship, and Border Crossings,* edited by Eithne Luibhéid and Lionel Cantú, NED-New ed., U of Minnesota P, 2005, pp. ix–xlvi.

Lyons, Scott Richard. "Rhetorical Sovereignty: What Do American Indians Want from Writing?" *College Composition and Communication,* vol. 51, no. 3, 2000, pp. 447–68.

Martin, Vivian B., et al. "What Is Grounded Theory Good For?" *Journalism & Mass Communication Quarterly,* vol. 95, no. 1, 2018, pp. 11–22. *Sage Journals,* https://doi.org/10.1177/1077699018759676.

Martinez, Aja Y. "'The American Way': Resisting the Empire of Force and Color-Blind Racism." *College English,* vol. 71, no. 6, 2009, pp. 584–95.

———. *Counterstory: The Rhetoric and Writing of Critical Race Theory.* Studies in Writing and Rhetoric, National Council of Teachers of English, 2020.

———. "Critical Race Theory: Its Origins, History, and Importance to the Discourses and Rhetorics of Race." *Frame,* vol. 27, no. 2, 2014, pp. 9–27.

Martínez, Óscar. *A History of Violence: Living and Dying in Central America.* Verso Books, 2016.

———. "Why the Children Fleeing Central America Will Not Stop Coming." *The Nation,* 30 July 2014, https://www.thenation.com/article/archive/why-children-fleeing-central-america-will-not-stop-coming/.

Matloff, Norman. "On the Need for Reform of the H-1B Non-Immigrant Work Visa in Computer-Related Occupations." *University of Michigan Journal of Law Reform,* vol. 36, no. 4, 2003, pp. 815–914.

Matsuda, Paul K. "The Myth of Linguistic Homogeneity in U.S. College Composition." *College English,* vol. 68, no. 6, 2006, pp. 637–51.

Mays, Kyle T. *An Afro-Indigenous History of the United States.* Beacon Press, 2021.

McIlwaine, Cathy, and Caroline O. N. Moser. "Violence and Social Capital in Urban Poor Communities: Perspectives from Colombia and Guatemala." *Journal of International Development,* vol. 13, no. 7, 2001, pp. 965–84.

Medina, Cruz. "Decolonial Potential in a Multilingual FYC." *Composition Studies,* vol. 47, no. 1, 2019, pp. 74–95.

———. "Digital Latinx Storytelling: Testimonio as Multi-Modal Resistance." *Racial Shorthand: Coded Discrimination Contested in Social Media,* edited by Cruz Medina and Octavio Pimentel, Computers and Composition Digital Press, Computers and Composition Digital Press / Utah State UP, 2018, http://ccdigitalpress.org/shorthand.

———. "The Family Profession." *College Composition and Communication,* vol. 65, no. 1, 2013, pp. 34–36.

Medina, Cruz, and Aja Y. Martinez. "Contexts of Lived Realities in SB 1070 Arizona." *Present Tense: A Journal of Rhetoric in Society,* vol. 4, no. 2, 2015, pp. 1–8.

Meghji, Ali. "Towards a Theoretical Synergy: Critical Race Theory and Decolonial Thought in Trumpamerica and Brexit Britain." *Current Sociology,* vol. 70, no. 5, 2020, pp. 1–18. *Sage Journals,* https://doi.org/10.1177/0011392120969764.

Menchú, Rigoberta. *I, Rigoberta Menchú: An Indian Woman in Guatemala.* Edited and introduced by Elisabeth Burgos-Debray, translated by Ann Wright, Verso Books, 2010.

Mignolo, Water. *The Darker Side of the Renaissance: Literacy, Territoriality, and Colonization.* U of Michigan P, 2003.

———. "Delinking: The Rhetoric of Modernity, the Logic of Coloniality and the Grammar of De-coloniality." *Cultural Studies,* vol. 21, no. 2–3, 2007, pp. 449–514.

Miller, James. "Get Ready for the 'Tech Alt-Right' to Gain Power and Influence in Silicon Valley." *Insider,* 9 Aug. 2017, https://businessinsider.com/get-ready-for-the-tech-alt-right-to-gain-influence-in-silicon-valley-2017-8.

Miranda, Jeanne, et al. "Depression Prevalence in Disadvantaged Young Black Women: African and Caribbean Immigrants Compared to US-Born African Americans." *Social Psychiatry and Psychiatric Epidemiology,* vol. 40, 2005, pp. 253–58.

Moss, Beverly J. *A Community Text Arises: A Literate Text and a Literacy Tradition in African-American Churches.* Hampton Press, 2003.

Moynihan, Donald, et al. "Kafka's Bureaucracy: Immigration Administrative Burdens in the Trump Era." *Perspectives on Public Management and Governance,* vol. 5, no. 1, 2022, pp. 22–35. *Oxford Academic,* https://doi.org/10.1093/ppmgov/gvab025.

Mukavetz, Andrea Riley. "Decolonial Theory and Methodology." *Composition Studies,* vol. 46, no. 1, 2018, pp. 124–93.

WORKS CITED • 143

Muwekma Ohlone Indian Tribe. "Response to the Department of the Interior, BAR/BIA Proposed Findings." 2002.

Neate, Rupert. "Donald Trump Doubles Down on Mexico 'Rapists' Comments Despite Outrage." *The Guardian,* 2 July 2015, https://theguardian.com/us-news/2015/jul/02/donald-trump-racist-claims-mexico-rapes.

Nijmeh, Charlene. "Political Erasure of the Muwekma Ohlone Tribe and the Complicity of Silence." *Daily Californian: Berkeley's News,* 5 Nov. 2021, https://www.dailycal.org/2021/11/05/political-erasure-of-the-muwekma-ohlone-tribe-and-the-complicity-of-silence.

Obinna, Denise N. "Seeking Sanctuary: Violence against Women in El Salvador, Honduras, and Guatemala." *Violence against Women,* vol. 27, no. 6/7, 2021, pp. 806–27.

Olivas, Michael A. "The Chronicles, My Grandfather's Stories, and Immigration Law: The Slave Traders' Chronicle as Racial History." *Critical Race Theory: The Cutting Edge,* edited by Richard Delgado, Temple UP, 1995, pp. 9–20.

Olson, Christa J. "But in Regard to These (the American) Continents: U.S. National Rhetorics and the Figure of Latin America." *Rhetoric Society Quarterly,* vol. 45, no. 3, 2015, pp. 264–77. *Taylor & Francis Online,* https://doi.org/10.1080/02773945.2015.1032857.

Ore, Ersula J. *Lynching: Violence, Rhetoric, and American Identity.* Mississippi UP, 2019.

Ovide, Shira. "Trump Win Is Silicon Valley's Loss on Immigration." *Bloomberg.com,* 9 Nov. 2016, https://bloomberg.com/gadfly/articles/2016-11-09/donald-trump-victory-is-silicon-valley-s-loss-on-immigration.

Padilla, Yajaira M. "The Central American Transnational Imaginary: Defining the Transnational and Gendered Contours of Central American Immigrant Experience." *Latino Studies,* vol. 11, no. 2, 2013, pp. 150–66.

Perkins, John. *Beyond Charity: The Call to Christian Community Development.* Baker Books, 1993.

Perryman-Clark, Staci M. "Who We Are(n't) Assessing: Racializing Language and Writing Assessment in Writing Program Administration." *College English,* vol. 79, no. 2, 2016, pp. 206–11.

Pimentel, Octavio. *Historias de Éxito Within Mexican Communities: Silenced Voices.* Palgrave Macmillan, 2015.

Pitti, Stephen J. *The Devil in Silicon Valley: Northern California, Race, and Mexican Americans.* Princeton UP, 2003.

Portes, Alejandro, and Lingxin Hao. "E Pluribus Unum: Bilingualism and Loss of Language in the Second Generation." *Sociology of Education,* vol. 71, no. 4, 1998, pp. 269–94.

Powell, M., et al. "Our Story Begins Here: Constellating Cultural Rhetorics." *enculturation: a journal of rhetoric, writing, and culture,* 25 Oct. 2014, https://enculturation.net/our-story-begins-here.

Puzo, Mario. *The Godfather.* Penguin, 2002.

Quinn, Michelle. "Tech's Foreign Workers Worry as They Await Trump Administration." *Mercury News,* 2 Dec. 2016, http://www.mercurynews.com/2016/12/02/techs-foreign-workers-worry-as-they-await-trump-administration/.

Rain Anderson, Joyce. "Remapping Settler Colonial Territories: Bringing Local Native Knowledge into the Classroom." *Survivance, Sovereignty, and Story: Teaching American Indian Rhetorics,* edited by Lisa King et al., Utah State UP, 2015, pp. 160–69.

Ramirez, Maria Liliana. "¡No Vengan! Immigration Art in the Post-Trump Era." *American Quarterly,* vol. 75 no. 1, 2023, p. 177–93. *Project MUSE,* https://doi.org/10.1353/aq.2023.0009.

WORKS CITED

Raney, Adam. "A Murder an Hour: El Salvador's Gang Violence Soars. *Al Jazeera,* 30 July 2015, https://www.aljazeera.com/features/2015/7/30/a-murder-an-hour-el-salvadors-gang-violence-soars.

Ribando, Clare M. *Gangs in Central America.* Congressional Research Service, 2007.

Ribero, Ana M. "Citizenship." *Decolonizing Rhetoric and Composition Studies: New Latinx Key Words for Theory and Pedagogy,* edited by Iris Ruiz and Raúl Sánchez, Palgrave Macmillan, 2016, pp. 31–46.

———. *Dreamer Nation: Immigration, Activism, and Neoliberalism.* U of Alabama P, 2023.

Ríos, Gabriela. "Cultivating Land-Based Literacies and Rhetorics." *Literacy in Composition Studies,* vol. 3, no. 1, 2015, pp. 60–70.

Rizzo, Salvador. "A Caravan of Phony Claims from the Trump Administration." *Washington Post,* 25 Oct. 2018, https://washingtonpost.com/politics/2018/10/25/caravan-phony-claims-trump-administration/.

Rodriguez Fielder, Elizabeth. "On Strike and On Stage: Migration, Mobilization, and the Cultural Work of El Teatro Campesino." *American Studies in Scandinavia,* vol. 46, no. 1, 2014, pp. 103–21.

Romero, Dennis. "Splitting California into 6 States? Fail." *LA Weekly,* 12 Sept. 2014, https://www.laweekly.com/splitting-california-into-6-states-fail/.

Romero, Mary. "Crossing the Immigration and Race Border: A Critical Race Theory Approach to Immigration Studies." *Contemporary Justice Review,* vol. 11, no. 1, 2008, pp. 23–37.

Romney, Lee. "Oakland Churches Offer Aid, Sanctuary to Central American Immigrants." *Los Angeles Times,* 30 Dec. 2014, https://latimes.com/local/california/la-me-bay-area-sanctuary-20141231-story.html.

Ross, Andrew S. "Great Divide in Silicon Valley's Wealth Grows Even Wider." *San Francisco Gate,* Hearst Communications, 5 Feb. 2014, https://www.sfgate.com/business/bottomline/article/Great-divide-in-Silicon-Valley-s-wealth-grows-5205029.php.

Ruiz, Iris D. *Reclaiming Composition for Chicano/as and Other Ethnic Minorities.* Palgrave Macmillan, 2016.

Sanford, Victoria. *Textures of Terror: The Murder of Claudina Isabel Velasquez and Her Father's Quest for Justice.* 1st ed., U of California P, 2023. California Series in Public Anthropology 55. *JSTOR,* https://doi.org/10.2307/jj.608347.

Schmidt, Paul W. "An Overview and Critique of US Immigration and Asylum Policies in the Trump Era." *Journal on Migration and Human Security,* vol. 7, no. 3, 2019, pp. 92–102.

Serviss, Tricia C. "Femicide and Rhetorics of Coadyuvante in Ciudad Juárez: Valuing Rhetorical Traditions in the Americas." *College English,* vol. 75, no. 6, 2013, pp. 608–28.

Shah, Rachael W. *Rewriting Partnerships: Community Perspectives on Community-Based Learning.* UP of Colorado, 2020.

Shahshahani, Azadeh, and Chiraayu Gosrani. "'Known Adversary': The Targeting of the Immigrants' Rights Movement in the Post-Trump Era." *Emory Law Journal,* vol. 72, 2022, pp. 1245–300.

Sin Nombre. Directed by Cary Joji Fukunaga, Universal Studios Home Entertainment, DVD, 2009.

Sittig, Ann L., and Martha Florinda González. *The Mayans among Us: Migrant Women and Meatpacking on the Great Plains.* U of Nebraska P, 2016.

Smith, Linda Tuhiwai. *Decolonizing Methodologies: Research and Indigenous Peoples.* Zed Books, 1999.

Soboroff, Jacob. "More than 2,100 Children Separated at Border 'Have Not Yet Been Reunified,' Biden Task Force Says." *NBC News,* 8 June 2021, https://www.nbcnews.com/politics/immigration/more-2-100-children-separated-border-have-not-yet-been-n1269918.

Solórzano, Daniel, and Dolores Delgado Bernal. "Examining Transformational Resistance through Critical Race and LatCrit Theory Framework: Chicana and Chicano Students in an Urban Context." *Urban Education,* vol. 36, no. 3, 2001, pp. 308–42.

Southern Poverty Law Center. "Family Separation: A Timeline." 23 Mar. 2022, https://www.splcenter.org/news/2022/03/23/family-separation-timeline.

Spiker, Steve, et al. *Homicides in Oakland/2008 Homicide Report: An Analysis of Homicides in Oakland from January through December, 2008.* Urban Strategies Council, 2009.

Taft-Morales, Maureen. *Guatemala: Political, Security, and Socio-Economic Conditions and U.S. Relations.* Congressional Research Service, 2014.

Taylor, Edward. "A Critical Race Analysis of the Achievement Gap in the United States: Politics, Reality, and Hope." *Leadership and Policy in Schools,* vol. 5, no. 1, 2006, pp. 71–87.

Taylor, Edward, et al., editors. *Foundations of Critical Race Theory in Education.* Routledge, 2009.

Thibodeau, Patrick, and Sharon Machlis. "The Data Shows: Top H-1B Users Are Offshore Outsourcers." *Computerworld,* 14 Feb. 2013, https://www.computerworld.com/article/2494926/technology-law-regulation-the-data-shows-top-h-1b-users-are-offshore-outsourcers.html.

Torres, John. *The Guatemalan Genocide of the Maya People (Bearing Witness).* The Rosen Publishing Group, 2018.

Toy, Sarah. "These Companies Are Expected to Profit from Trump's Continued 'Zero-Tolerance' Policy at the Border." *MarketWatch,* 25 June 2018, https://marketwatch.com/story/these-companies-are-expected-to-profit-from-trumps-continued-zero-tolerance-policy-at-the-border-2018-06-22.

"Tuition and Fees." *City College of San Francisco,* https://www.ccsf.edu/admissions-recordsregistration/tuition-and-fees.

Ujpán, Ignacio Bizarro, narrator. *Joseño: Another Mayan Voice Speaks from Guatemala.* Edited and translated by James D. Sexton, New Mexico UP, 2001.

Urrea, Luis A. *Devil's Highway: A True Story.* Back Bay Books, 2008.

Valenzuela, Angela. *Subtractive Schooling: U.S.-Mexican Youth and the Politics of Caring.* State U of New York P, 1999.

Villanueva, Victor. *Bootstraps: From an American Academic of Color.* National Council of Teachers of English, 1993.

Walia, Harsha. *Border and Rule: Global Migration, Capitalism, and the Rise of Racist Nationalism.* Haymarket Books, 2021.

Wane, Njoki N. "Indigenous Education and Cultural Resistance: A Decolonizing Project." *Curriculum Inquiry,* vol. 39, no. 1, 2009, pp. 159–78.

Wang, Amy B. "Donald Trump Plans to Immediately Deport 2 Million to 3 Million Undocumented Immigrants." *Washington Post,* 14 Nov. 2016, washingtonpost.com/news/the-fix/wp/2016/11/13/donald-trump-plans-to-immediately-deport-2-to-3-million-undocumented-immigrants/?utm_term=.2d773ce3834d.

Wilde, Oscar. *The Critic as Artist.* David Zwirner Books, 2019.

Wingard, Jennifer. "Trump's Not Just One Bad Apple: He's the Product of a Spoiled Bunch." *Faking the News: What Rhetoric Can Teach Us about Donald J. Trump,* edited by Ryan Skinnell. Imprint Academic, 2018, pp. 43–57. *ProQuest Ebook Central,* https://ebookcentral.proquest.com/lib/santaclara/detail.action?docID=5437569.

Winton, Ailsa. "Urban Violence: A Guide to the Literature." *Environment and Urbanization,* vol. 16, no. 2, 2004, pp. 165–84.

———. "Youth, Gangs and Violence: Analysing the Social and Spatial Mobility of Young People in Guatemala City." *Children's Geographies,* vol. 3, no. 2, 2005, pp. 167–84. *Taylor & Francis Online,* https://doi.org/10.1080/14733280500161537.

Wolfe, Patrick. "Settler Colonialism and the Elimination of the Native." *Journal of Genocide Research,* vol. 8, no. 4, 2006, 387–409. *Taylor & Francis Online,* https://doi.org/10.1080/14623520601056240.

World Bank. "Annual Report 2015." World Bank Group, 2015, https://www.worldbank.org/en/about/annual-report-2015.

Yosso, Tara J. *Critical Race Counterstories along the Chicana/Chicano Educational Pipeline.* Routledge, 2013.

Young, Morris. *Minor Re/visions: Asian American Literacy Narratives as a Rhetoric of Citizenship.* Southern Illinois UP, 2004.

Zur, Judith N. *Violent Memories: Mayan War Widows in Guatemala.* Westview Press, 1998.

INDEX

activism, 6

Afro-pessimism, 52

American Dream, 18, 32, 38–39, 80, 93, 126. See also *superarse*

anti-Latinx legislation, ix, 19

antimigrant policy, 3

Anzaldúa, Gloria, xi

Arizona, ix, 19, 59–60

assimilation, 39, 73, 96

bad migrant, 9, 31, 35, 87

Bay Area, 9, 27, 35, 39, 91, 127. See also California; East Bay; Silicon Valley

Bell, Derrick, 13, 31, 50, 51, 93

Biden, Joseph, 60–61, 106

bilingual education, 17, 87, 92

"build a wall" rhetoric, 35, 60

Bush, George W., 6

California, 20; community college, 115, 119

campesino farmworkers, 12, 23, 78, 97, 109–10, 117–18, 121

Catholic Church, ix, 28–29, 70

Catholic mission, 27

citizenship, 13–14, 26–27, 31–32, 38, 43, 51, 54

civil war / *la violencia* (Guatemala), vii, 3, 4, 5, 10, 11, 12, 14, 21, 28, 47, 64–67, 72–73, 75–76, 90, 100–101, 118

colonialism, 47, 51

Conedera, Bishop Juan Gerardi, 28

Costanoan, 33. *See also* Ohlone and Muwekma

counterstory, 13, 22, 110

critical race theory (CRT), x, 17, 18, 21, 22, 31, 40, 44, 47, 50, 60, 85, 95; and education policy, 51, 102; and methodology, 22

culture of learned distrust, 25, 101

culture of silence, 19, 21, 71–72, 76

decolonial: critical race theory, 20–21, 40, 43–44, 45–46, 95; knowledge, 17; methodologies, 16, 55–56, 68, 94; pedagogy, 113–14; research methods, 55–56, 69; tenets of CRT, 45–46; theory, x, 14, 60, 95

decolonizing, viii

delinking, 46–47

Department of Homeland Security, 6

148 · INDEX

deportation, 2, 13, 60, 79–80, 96–97, 120

displacement, 29, 51, 65, 86, 87, 90, 121

disposable labor, 12–13, 98, 109

dominant narrative, 49, 106, 116–18, 121. *See also* majoritarian stories; stock stories

Draper, Tim, 91

drug traffickers, 9–10, 38, 77, 82, 97. *See also* narcos

East Bay, 48, 79, 82, 95; violence in, 108, 112

education policy, 19, 51. *See also* English official; English-only; Proposition 187

El Salvador, 63; and civil war, 63–64; violence in, 75, 82

English language: education, 20, 108, 116; learners, 18; literacy, 13–14, 39, 117–18

English official, 91–92. *See also* English-only

English-only, 86, 89, 91–92, 99. *See also* English official

exclusion: economy of, 18, 20, 28–29, 40, 82; history of, 32–33. *See also* free market: economy

experiential knowledge, 44, 46, 53, 111

felt need, 96

femicide, 66, 74, 75, 76

Foreign Miners' Tax, 34

Francis (pope), 20, 28–30

free market: capitalism, 47–48, 78–79; economy, 38. *See also* exclusion: economy of

gender-based violence, 19, 21, 66, 72–77

generational trauma, 4, 21, 125. *See also* culture of silence; trauma

genocide, 5, 47, 65, 74, 76, 90. *See also* scorched earth campaigns

gentrification, 15, 30, 39, 51, 87

good migrant, 35–36

grounded theory, 20–21, 43, 45, 95

Guatemala, 46–47, 51, 60–61, 66–67, 71, 72, 96, 99, 101; army of, 73; government of, 65–66, 71, 90; and guerillas, 73; and illiteracy, 70, 117–18

H-1B visas, 20, 27, 36–37

Harris, Kamala, 5, 10, 60–61

haunting, ix, 71

I, Rigoberta Menchú, (Menchú), 11

immigration, 12, 67; and Bible, 8, 28; and criminalization, 38, 79; decolonial understanding of, 67, 74; denationalization of, 70; policy, 20, 59, 67; Reform and Control Act, 35; system, 38

indentured servitude, 36–37

Indigenous: education, 114, 117, 119; Guatemalans, 30, 46, 51–52, 101, 109; knowledge, 56; land, 87, 91, 102; language, 18, 94; Maya students, 4, 25, 32, 61, 69, 90

interdisciplinarity, 52

interest convergence, 48–49

intersectionality, 50

Jesuit: immersion trip, 81, 128; university, 28

Jim Crow, 13

la violencia. See civil war / *la violencia*

Ladino, 47, 49, 90; ideology, 73

land-based literacies, 14

LatCrit, 17, 111

lease, 84–86

"learn the language," 5, 40, 58, 93, 97, 106, 110, 129

Leviticus, 28

linguicism, 18, 86, 89, 106. *See also* linguistic discrimination

linguistic discrimination, 9, 86, 89, 92, 105. *See also* linguicism

lived experience, 17, 68, 111. *See also* experiential knowledge

loci of enunciation, 111

lynching, 34

majoritarian stories, 13, 22, 56, 109–11, 118–20

Mam, 22, 58, 65, 94, 96, 99–101. *See also* Indigenous: language

Manifest Destiny, 33, 91

Mara Salvatrucha. *See* MS-13

maras (street gangs), 77–78, 80, 82, 121

Maya, 3–4, 11, 14, 21, 25, 46–47, 49, 51–52, 58, 61, 64–73, 87–88, 90, 93–94, 99–101, 109, 117–18. *See also* Indigenous: Guatemalans

Mayan language, 22, 101. *See also* Mam

Menchú, Rigoberta, 11, 14, 90

mestizaje, x

Mignolo, Walter, 15, 47

migrants, 12–13; and caravans, 26, 42, 67, 80; and depression, 103; and victimization, 109, 120

Mission District, 8, 38, 39

missionaries: goals of, 104; outreach of, 7–8

monolingual ideology, 9, 18, 87, 99, 106

MS-13, 5, 26, 42–43, 63, 80–81

multilingualism, 98. *See also* plurilingualism

narcos, 77, 78. *See also* drug traffickers

National Foundation for American Policy, 35

North American Free Trade Agreement (NAFTA), 66

neocolonialism, 12, 14–15, 19–21, 36, 40, 42–43, 46–47, 51, 64, 79, 87

Obama, Barack, 2, 24, 79, 120

objective research, 56, 110

Ohlone and Muwekma, 27, 33

participant observation, 19

pedagogy, 108, 113–14, 122–23

plurilingualism, 118. *See also* multilingualism

pluriversal, 45, 52, 111–12

positionality of researcher, 70

prayer requests, 58, 71, 86, 102–3

property, 15, 22, 31, 50–51, 54, 87, 91, 93; and Sanctuary lease, 19, 22, 84, 88, 94, 104–5, 123, 129

Proposition 187, 31, 34, 112, 116

racial discrimination, 13

racism, 14, 47, 110; and colonization, 67

reciprocity, 25, 69

refuge, 2, 5–6, 9–10, 12, 40, 42–43, 54, 67, 94, 102

reparations, 50

rhetoric of immigration, 3

rhetorical study, 68

Sanctuary: church, 2, 8, 17, 27, 41, 62, 68, 85 fig. 1; English program, 18, 24–25, 70, 72, 74, 102–4, 107–8; lease, 19, 22, 84, 88, 94, 104–5, 123, 129

sanctuary effort, 7

Santa Barbara Independent, ix

Santa Barbara seminary ix

Santa Clara University, vii, ix

school segregation, 13, 93–94, 98

scorched earth campaigns, 67, 73, 74. *See also* genocide

"secure our borders" rhetoric, 5, 9, 43, 60

self-determination, 113

separation of migrant families, 31, 46, 103, 120, 126. *See also* "zero tolerance"

settler colonialism, 14–15, 18, 50, 91

sexual assault, 72, 74–77, 80–81

Silicon Valley, 3, 9, 10, 27, 30, 35–37, 40, 91, 127; and diversity, 37

Sin Nombre, 80

slavery, 13, 48–51, 36

social justice, 54

sovereignty, 49, 70

Spanish language, 91, 99–100

Standard Academic English, 98, 120

stock stories, 13, 22, 49, 109, 111, 117, 120. *See also* majoritarian stories

storytelling, 53–54

subtractive curriculum, 114

superarse, 80, 93, 95. *See also* American Dream

surveys, 57–58, 70–71, 74

Tenderloin District, 7, 12, 38

testimonio, 111. *See also* counterstory

textbook, 114. *See also* workbook

throwaway culture, 28–29. *See also* exclusion: economy of

translation, 16

transnational business, cost of, 67, 76–77

trauma, 14, 21, 72–73, 76, 79–80, 103, 125–26

150 · INDEX

Trump, Donald: and birther claims, 1, 24; executive order of, 6, 126; policy of, 17, 19, 31, 42 (*see also* "zero tolerance"); presidential campaign, 1, 21, 34, 35, 44, 60, 79, 93, 127; rhetoric of, 108, 121; and social media, 4–5, 10, 26, 42

US Constitution, 17, 31, 51, 91
US intervention, 51
US-Mexican War, 33
US-Mexico border, 66, 81

violence, 21, 43, 65; in Central America, 61, 63–64, 66, 75; in Guatemala, 16, 66, 72, 74–76, 78, 113, 121. *See also* femicide; gender-based violence; sexual assault

volunteer labor, 8, 13, 25, 55, 70, 97, 102, 108–9, 113, 122–23, 129–30
vulnerable population, 70

white nationalist ideology, 37, 60, 79, 86
white supremacist: ideology, 49, 89, 106; policy, 43
whiteness as property, 13, 31, 50, 85
Wilde, Oscar, viii
workbook, 99, 102, 113–14

xenophobic ideology, 86

"zero tolerance," 17, 19, 31, 46, 126. *See also* Trump policy

GLOBAL LATIN/O AMERICAS

FREDERICK LUIS ALDAMA AND LOURDES TORRES, SERIES EDITORS

This series focuses on the Latino experience in its totality as set within a global dimension. The series showcases the variety and vitality of the presence and significant influence of Latinos in the shaping of the culture, history, politics and policies, and language of the Americas—and beyond. It welcomes scholarship regarding the arts, literature, philosophy, popular culture, history, politics, law, history, and language studies, among others.

Sanctuary: Exclusion, Violence, and Indigenous Migrants in the East Bay
  CRUZ MEDINA

Everyday Dirty Work: Invisibility, Communication, and Immigrant Labor
  WILFREDO ALVAREZ

Building Confianza: Empowering Latinos/as Through Transcultural Health Care Communication
  DALIA MAGAÑA

Fictions of Migration: Narratives of Displacement in Peru and Bolivia
  LORENA CUYA GAVILANO

Baseball as Mediated Latinidad: Race, Masculinity, Nationalism, and Performances of Identity
  JENNIFER DOMINO RUDOLPH

False Documents: Inter-American Cultural History, Literature, and the Lost Decade (1975–1992)
  FRANS WEISER

Public Negotiations: Gender and Journalism in Contemporary US Latina/o Literature
  ARIANA E. VIGIL

Democracy on the Wall: Street Art of the Post-Dictatorship Era in Chile
  GUISELA LATORRE

Gothic Geoculture: Nineteenth-Century Representations of Cuba in the Transamerican Imaginary
  IVONNE M. GARCÍA

Affective Intellectuals and the Space of Catastrophe in the Americas
  JUDITH SIERRA-RIVERA

Spanish Perspectives on Chicano Literature: Literary and Cultural Essays
  EDITED BY JESÚS ROSALES AND VANESSA FONSECA

Sponsored Migration: The State and Puerto Rican Postwar Migration to the United States
  EDGARDO MELÉNDEZ

La Verdad: An International Dialogue on Hip Hop Latinidades
  EDITED BY MELISSA CASTILLO-GARSOW AND JASON NICHOLS

www.ingramcontent.com/pod-product-compliance
Lightning Source LLC
Chambersburg PA
CBHW030757090425
24824CB00001B/13